Furniture Design *and* Construction *for the* Interior Designer

D0084379

Furniture Design *and* Construction *for the* Interior Designer

CHRISTOPHER NATALE

The Art Institute of Phoenix

Fairchild Books

New York

Executive Editor: Olga T. Kontzias
Acquisitions Editor: Joseph Miranda
Editorial Development Director: Jennifer Crane
Associate Art Director: Erin Fitzsimmons
Production Director: Ginger Hillman
Production Editor: Jessica Rozler
Project Manager, Development: Patricia Shogren, GEX Publishing Services
Project Manager: Jeff Hoffman
Copyeditor: Nina Hnatov
Cover Design: Mike Suh
Cover Art: iStockPhoto
Text Design and Page Composition: Andrew Katz
Illustrations and photographs: Christopher Natale

Library of Congress Catalog Card Number: 2008924428
ISBN-13: 978-1-56367-565-2
GST R 133004424

Printed in the United States of America
TP09

Contents

Extended Contents

Introduction

The purpose of this book is to satisfy the need in the interior design field for a source that teaches the aesthetics as well as the construction of residential furniture. This book uses historic and contemporary design examples to show how styles have changed through the years. Part I covers the tools needed to design furniture including furniture styles, the design process, basic materials, hardware, joinery, and finishes. Part II breaks down the construction of furniture based on the characteristics of each space and illustrates how to engineer different types of furniture through step-by-step processes with visual examples. Interior designers will learn to create drawings with confidence and how to explain these drawings to a client or custom builder.

This book was created with the interior designer in mind. Therefore, instead of showing how to build a particular type of furniture, it teaches how furniture is constructed as a whole and what is expected of the interior designer.

Readers are introduced to the history of furniture in the United States and are shown how to sketch and render furniture. Other chapters describe the different types of materials and how some furniture dimensions can be dictated by these materials. The book also explains how furniture is joined together as well as the various types of finishing processes.

Because interior designers organize and create livable spaces, the second part of this book is broken down by room, showing how pieces are constructed for particular spaces. Understanding the basic construction of furniture greatly increases the success of the design. Because interior designers typically do not build the furniture themselves, this book shows how drawings are created so that a custom builder will be able to create the interior designer's vision. By the end of this book, an interior designer should be confident in designing pieces of furniture as well as in understanding what is involved in the construction of those pieces. This book emphasizes custom furniture design and fabrication and is geared toward residential design. Nonresidential design typically uses furniture systems. Designing furniture systems is completely different from custom designing because of the production and shipping aspects as well as the types of materials and finishes.

The illustrations in this book show all aspects of furniture design and construction by illustrating basic joinery, section views, and complete pieces. Many of these illustrations show different types of drawings and exploded views. Along with the drawings are photos of details and completed pieces of furniture.

Design Philosophy

My approach to design is to treat furniture as pieces of functional sculpture. In addition to its utilitarian purpose, a piece of furniture should also serve as an artistic focal point or perhaps as an accent in a large design space. Using the scale and proportions of the human form as a starting point, I determine the rough sizes and dimensions of the piece. From there, aesthetics and materials enter the creative process as I experiment with various combinations and possibilities. Creative decisions are informed by the original ergonomic vision so that the finished piece will combine the highest artistic standards with optimum comfort and functionality for the end user.

Furniture design is my primary creative outlet because it satisfies my twin passions for the conceptual journey of the artistic process and the hands-on work of shaping the finished piece. My designs are influenced by classic ideas of form and proportion, by the properties of raw materials, and by the intended application of the completed product. My work as a designer is to combine all of these ingredients in an innovative way to provide both visual delight and physical comfort. The forms of sailboats and aircraft inspire many of my designs, not only for their graceful lines, but also for the pleasing harmony they offer between form and function.

Teaching Philosophy

My five-step teaching philosophy, which I use in the classroom, is designed to enable the richest possible learning experience for students who desire to pursue an art-related calling.

- ▸ Step 1: Set a clearly stated learning objective. Students need to understand how a lesson or exercise relates to a particular principle or technique.
- ▸ Step 2: Provide an inspiring mix of completed professional or student projects as visual examples. The mental connection between finished pieces and the desired learning objective is critical because art is a visual process.
- ▸ Step 3: Offer a creative problem-solving demonstration. To avoid becoming overwhelmed or discouraged in the beginning, students need a conceptual or technical path to follow from blank media to a completed exercise.
- ▸ Step 4: Create a hands-on activity that leads students through a trial-and-error process that allows them to create their own solutions.
- ▸ Step 5: Operate with the recognition that each student is an individual artist and not subject to a creative formula.

Evaluation of an artistic learning experience must consider individual effort and growth in addition to talent.

Acknowledgments

I would like to start by thanking four teachers who over the years have helped to shape my design style and confidence. The first is George Landino, who showed me that it's still possible to create unique and interesting designs as well as giving me a foundation in fabrication. Karen Thomas and Tom Muir, from my time at the College for Creative Studies, pushed me on perfecting the technique, fabrication, and concepts behind my designs and gave me the ability to create hundreds of drawings from a simple idea. The late Dave Pimentel, my teacher at Arizona State University, helped me begin to produce a completely new way of designing and creating furniture.

I would also like to thank everyone who worked on the book at Fairchild Books, including Joseph Miranda, the acquisitions editor who helped me start this whole process; Laura Lawrie, the developmental editor; Patricia Shogren; and Jennifer Crane, the senior development editor who all helped organize and refine the book.

A special thanks goes to my wife Nicole and our friend Toni Ackley for their creative input, energy, and support. I also want to thank my fellow colleagues, students, and friends at The Art Institute of Phoenix, particularly Carol Morrow, Bob Adams, Maryse Jospitre, Peter Halifax, Alex Simon, and Cindy Stedman. Finally, I thank May Dunn-Palensky for giving me the opportunity to teach and share my furniture experience with the students.

Tools for Designing Furniture

PART I

CHAPTER 1

Styles of Furniture

THE FIRST PART of this chapter provides a basic overview of the different styles of furniture that have influenced American design, starting with the Gothic period (1150–1550) through to Mid-Century Modern (1940–1960). This chapter also shows how different countries and regions, from England to France, Germany, and Scandinavia, influenced design. These influences then created "periods," such as the Victorian era, which then led into other completely different styles such as the Arts and Crafts movement. Illustrations are included for many of these periods to show how some furniture pieces from each era looked.

The second part of this chapter describes and shows examples of different types of furniture. Different versions of the same types of pieces are provided so that students can visually compare the styles.

Fig. 1.1

Fig. 1.2

Major Furniture Styles That Influenced American Design

The following furniture styles are organized chronologically, though the time periods of some styles may overlap; for example, Jacobean (1603–1690) and Louis XIII (1610–1643) overlap because these styles were created in two different countries, England and France. The furniture styles are presented in chronological order because in many cases one era influenced another by using elements of the previous designs or creating a completely new style as a rebellion against the previous era.

Gothic (1150–1550, revived in the nineteenth century) This architectural style was a major influence in furniture design. The most recognizable element from this era is the Gothic arc, which is an arc that creates a pointed top. (See Figure 1.1.)

Elizabethan (1558–1603) This style is named after Queen Elizabeth I of England. The Elizabethan style is not a unified classic style, but many pieces created in this style have an architectural quality to them. (See Figure 1.2.)

Renaissance (1460–1600, revived in the nineteenth century) This style came from Italy and was a reaction to the Gothic style. The furniture is functional with carvings and scrollwork. The revival pieces from 1850 to 1880 used the same details and were typically made from walnut.

Pilgrim (1550–1600) This functional American furniture style drew on influences from England. Made from New England trees in areas where the Pilgrims settled, the furniture is large and heavy. Pieces were built with a limited amount of tools that Pilgrims had brought with them. The early pieces were held together with pegs because nails and glue were scarce.

Jacobean (1603–1690) This type of furniture came from England and was what early American furniture was modeled on. It has dark finishes and mixes straight lines with ornate carving. (See Figure 1.3.)

Louis XIII (1610–1643) This French furniture has a massive, heavy feel and look to it, with carving and turning. Two distinct features of this style are the use of geometric panels with molding and elaborate turnings for the chairs and tables. (See Figure 1.4.)

Louis XIV (1643–1715) This furniture style built on the Louis XIII style. This era in France saw extravagant living within royalty and the upper class. One main feature of the Louis XIV style is the X-style stretcher to the chairs and other pieces. The image shown is a chair with a single straight stretcher. (See Figure 1.5.)

Early American (1640–1700) This style is basic and utilitarian. This New World furniture was made from local woods and was largely based on European styles from England, France, and Spain.

Fig. 1.3

Fig. 1.4

Fig. 1.5

Fig. 1.6

Fig. 1.7

Fig. 1.8

Fig. 1.9

William and Mary (1690–1725) This style gets its name from King William and Queen Mary, joint rulers of England (1689–1694). This furniture typically features turned legs with a Spanish or drake foot detail and was made from walnut. During this period new types of furniture developed, the most important example being the secretary, which incorporated a bookcase and a desk with a fall-front writing surface. (See Figure 1.6.)

Queen Anne (1700–1755) This style, which is still popular today, gets its name from Queen Anne of England (1702–1714). Two main elements of this furniture are the cabriole leg, which creates a light and graceful feel, and the pad foot. (See Figure 1.7.)

Louis XV (1715–1774) The eighteenth century saw changing social times in France, and changes in style as well. The early years of the Louis XV period were influenced by the Louis XIV style and picked up details like the X-style stretcher. But the details were more refined, with the use of cabriole legs and delicate carvings. (See Figure 1.8.)

Louis XVI (1774–1789) At this time, France moved to a simpler style; the curved lines of the legs were changed and became rigid turned details, and the backs of chairs used simple ovals and circles. (See Figure 1.9.)

Colonial (1700–1780) This style combined elements from William and Mary, Queen Anne, and Chippendale—which all started in England—to create a simplified style in the United States. (See Figure 1.10.)

Georgian (1714–1760) The name for this style comes from the reign of George I, king of England from 1714 to 1727, and from the reign of George II, who ruled from 1727 to 1760. This style is a more ornate version of the Queen Anne style. It has larger proportions, carving, and cabriole legs with a pad or ball and claw foot. (See Figure 1.11.)

Pennsylvania Dutch (1729–1830) This is a simple, straight, clean-line style of furniture based on function. Many of these pieces feature light to dark brown stains or colorful folk painting that was typical of German craftsmanship. (See Figure 1.12.)

Chippendale (1750–1790) The name comes from Thomas Chippendale, a British cabinetmaker and designer. He published his designs in *The Gentleman and Cabinet-Maker's Direction* in England in 1754. Chippendale incorporated many different influences into his designs. Today, Chippendale furniture is some of the most sought after by antique collectors. (See Figure 1.13.)

Fig. 1.10

Fig. 1.11

Fig. 1.12

Fig. 1.13

Fig. 1.14

Fig. 1.16

Fig. 1.15

Adam (1760–1790) This style of furniture is named after British architect and designer Robert Adam. The pieces from this era typically have rectilinear forms with inlaid decoration, applied classical motifs, and sometimes painted surfaces.

Hepplewhite (1765–1800) This style is named after George Hepplewhite, whose designs were published in *The Cabinet-Maker and Upholsterer's Guide* in England in 1788. The features of this furniture are its delicate elements such as tapered legs, veneers, and inlay. (See Figure 1.14.)

Federal (1780–1820) This furniture style from the United States combines both Hepplewhite and Sheraton, with straight clean lines, tapered legs, and inlay. (See Figure 1.15.)

Sheraton (1780–1820) This style is named after the British furniture designer Thomas Sheraton, whose designs were published in *The Cabinet Maker and Upholsterer's Drawing Book* in 1791 and can still be bought today. His designs influenced both English and American furniture designers. This neoclassical furniture has straight lines and contrasting veneers with shell inlaid decoration. (See Figure 1.16.)

Empire (1800–1840) Influenced by the French Empire style, this American style has dark finishes with graceful lines and strong proportions, creating a solid look and feel to the furniture. (See Figure 1.17.)

Shaker (1820–1860) This is a simple, functional style. Some common details are tapered legs, ladder-back chairs with contrasting woven seats, and simple wooden knobs. (See Figure 1.18.)

Biedermeier (1815–1848) This German style of furniture typically uses blond woods combined with architectural details. This style has curved lines and contrasting features. The name Biedermeier is not from a designer, but from two German words combined: "bieder," meaning common or plain, and "Meier," which is a common surname in Germany. This functional furniture has a simple style and was designed for the middle class. (See Figure 1.19.)

Victorian (1840–1910) Named after Queen Victoria of England (1837–1901), this style marked the beginning of the machine age, which saw the creation of the first mass-produced furniture. This style has graceful curved lines featuring upholstered sofas with exposed wood frames adding a contrast between the fabric and frame. (See Figure 1.20.)

Fig. 1.17

Fig. 1.18

Fig. 1.19

Fig. 1.20

Fig. 1.21

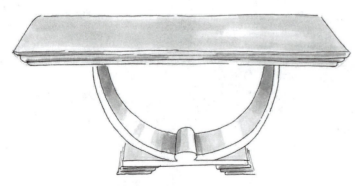

Fig. 1.22

Fig. 1.23

Arts and Crafts (1880–1910) This style, also known as Mission style, was a rebellion against Victorian industrialism in the United States. This handcrafted furniture emphasizes construction, using the joinery as a major design element. (See Figure 1.21.)

Art Nouveau (1890–1910) This style was a continued reaction against the Victorian era. This style originated in France and features flowing curves and detailed patterns. (See Figure 1.22.)

Art Deco (1920–1940) This style had a big impact on architecture, automobile design, clothing, and graphic design as well as furniture. It uses inlay with curves while creating different surface planes as well as creating a balance between positive and negative space. (See Figure 1.23.)

Mid-Century Modern (1940–1960) It can be argued that the Mid-Century Modern style actually began early in the twentieth century, or even earlier, with the Michael Thonet chair No. 14 (1859). This chair was a simple design with curved wood, which made it easy to reproduce at that time. This was one of the first mass-produced pieces of furniture. The Industrial Revolution made it possible to take a designer's original idea and, instead of creating just a few pieces, mass-produce the furniture, creating thousands of the same piece. Then, Bauhaus continued with the mass production of steel-designed furniture before World War II. Postwar technologies allowed new materials to be used, such as molded plywood and fiberglass in Charles and Ray Eames's designs and cast aluminum in Eero Saarinen's work. Most of the designs from this era are still produced today because of their simplicity and their functional details. (See Figure 1.24.)

Scandinavian Design (1930–1950) This style of furniture, which has also been called Contemporary, came from Denmark and Sweden and typically uses natural woods, veneers, and fiberglass.

Fig. 1.24

Fig. 1.25a Armchair

Fig. 1.25b Side chair

Fig. 1.25c Ladder-back chair

Fig. 1.26 Shaker-style rocker

Types of Furniture

Many of the types of furniture discussed in this section are covered in subsequent chapters, which show the complete construction and design as well as the typical dimensions of these pieces. The images provided in this section show the basic forms of the different furniture types in various styles.

Chairs

Chairs can be classified in many different ways including by era, style, or function. The chairs are listed here by function: the dining chair, the rocker or rocking chair, the lounge chair, and the sofa. Some of these pieces are designed with exposed wood frames, whereas others are typically completely upholstered.

DINING CHAIR

The basic design of the dining chair is derived, like all furniture, from the proportions of the human body; however, the design of dining chairs is also derived from the dining table. For example, each end of the table will have an armchair, and the sides of the table will have side chairs. The armchair and the side chair typically are duplicates of each other with the obvious distinction that one has arms and one does not. (See Figures 1.25a and 1.25b.) A popular type of dining chair is the ladder-back chair, which takes its name from the style of the back of the chair. (See Figure 1.25c.)

ROCKER

The rocker or rocking chair is simply a chair with a curved rail attached to the bottom of each side of the chair allowing it to rock back and forth. These chairs can be similar in style to a dining or lounge chair design. Figure 1.26 shows a Shaker-style rocking chair.

LOUNGE CHAIR

The lounge chair typically is wider than a dining chair and is used in the living room or family room. The styles of lounge chairs vary widely based on the style of the space for which they are designed. Two French styles are the Fauteuil (Figure 1.27a), which is an open arm chair, and the Bergère (Figure 1.27b), which is a closed arm chair.

Another type of French chair is the chaise longue, sometimes called the chaise lounge, which is a lounge chair on which the seat has been stretched to accommodate a person's extended legs. (See Figure 1.28.)

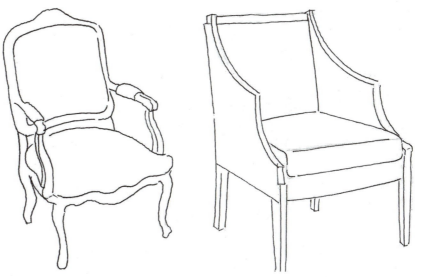

Fig. 1.27a Fauteuil   **Fig. 1.27b** Bergère

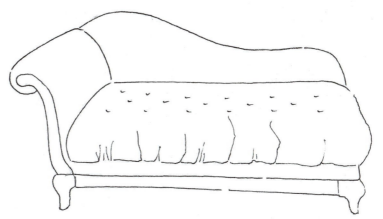

Fig. 1.28 Chaise longue

1.29 Windsor chair

Fig. 1.30a Wingback chair

Fig. 1.30b Club chair

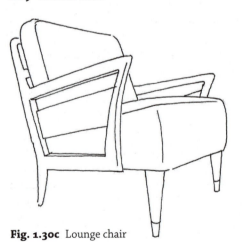

Fig. 1.30c Lounge chair

Fig. 1.30d Armless lounge

Fig. 1.30e Ottoman

Most lounge chairs will have some type of upholstery. A notable exception is the Windsor chair, which can be designed to be a dining chair, rocker, or lounge chair depending on the proportions of the chair. (See Figure 1.29.)

Some other popular lounge chair designs are the wing-back chair (Figure 1.30a), which is typically a taller style of chair with upholstered wings; the club chair (Figure 1.30b), which is a completely upholstered chair; and the arm and armless lounge chairs (Figures 1.30c and 1.30d). An ottoman (Figure 1.30e) often accompanies some types of lounge chairs as a foot stool.

Sofas

The lounge chair typically is an accent piece in a living room or family room where the dominant piece is the sofa or love seat. A sofa is an upholstered piece of furniture that will seat at least three persons, whereas a love seat is the same as the sofa but is smaller to accommodate seating for two. (See Figures 1.31a and 1.31b.) Another type of love seat or small couch is the settee, which, depending on the style, can be more like a bench. (See Figure 1.31c.) This piece typically can be found in the front hall or foyer of a large modern home.

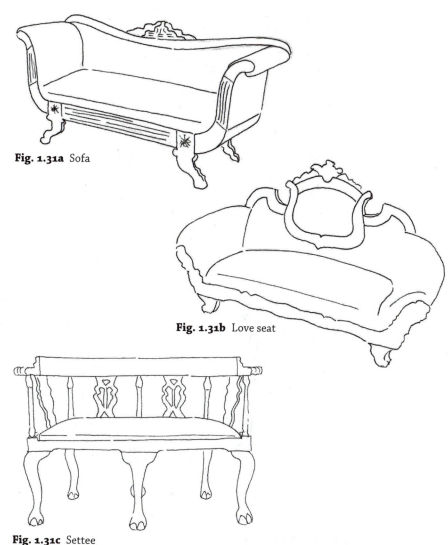

Fig. 1.31a Sofa

Fig. 1.31b Love seat

Fig. 1.31c Settee

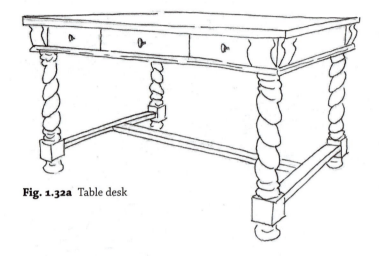

Fig. 1.32a Table desk

Fig. 1.32b Kneehole desk

Fig. 1.32c Rolltop desk

Fig. 1.32d Secretary desk

Desks

The desk has gone through many changes over the years, mainly because of changes in its function and in technology. Two standard desk styles have been the table desk and kneehole desk. (See Figures 1.32a and 1.32b.) The table desk is constructed like a table, but with small drawers below the top. The kneehole desk is designed with more drawer storage on each side. Two other common desk styles are the rolltop desk and the secretary desk. (See Figures 1.32c and 1.32d.) The rolltop desk is a larger type of desk that has wood material that can roll down to close off the top of the desk. The secretary desk is a smaller desk with a front panel that folds down to create the work surface. The purpose of both of these pieces is to be able to lock the desk's top when not in use.

Dressers

Dressers are designed for storage in the bedroom, typically with multiple drawers. The type of dresser is based on the arrangement of the drawers; for example, a chest of drawers is a vertical stacking of drawers, whereas a standard dresser has the drawers arranged horizontally. A highboy is a vertical design with long legs at the base, creating a delicate look. (See Figures 1.33a through d.)

Fig. 1.33a Dresser with mirror

Fig. 1.33b Chest of drawers

Fig. 1.33c Chest on chest

Fig. 1.33d Highboy—Chippendale

Fig. 1.34a Buffet

Fig. 1.34b China cabinet—Gothic

Fig. 1.34c Hutch

Fig. 1.34d Breakfront

Fig. 1.34e Console

Fig. 1.34f Pie safe

Dining Room Cabinetry

The cabinetry in the dining room can be broken down into two types: pieces designed for storage and pieces designed for display and storage. A buffet or sideboard is designed for storage and typically has drawers and doors, while the top can be used for serving. A china cabinet is designed much like a buffet but has a top cabinet with glass paneled doors for displaying items. (See Figures 1.34a through f.)

Tables

Tables are designed for a particular function. The size of the table and the tabletop height dictate its function. The dining table needs to be large enough to accommodate multiple persons, with a tabletop height around 29 to 30 inches. A coffee table, in comparison, is much smaller and has a tabletop height of about 15 inches. All of the tables shown here will be covered in more detail in subsequent chapters. (See Figures 1.35a through d and 1.36a through e.)

Fig. 1.35a Dining table

Fig. 1.35b Pedestal table

Fig. 1.35c Drop leaf table

Fig. 1.35d Gateleg table

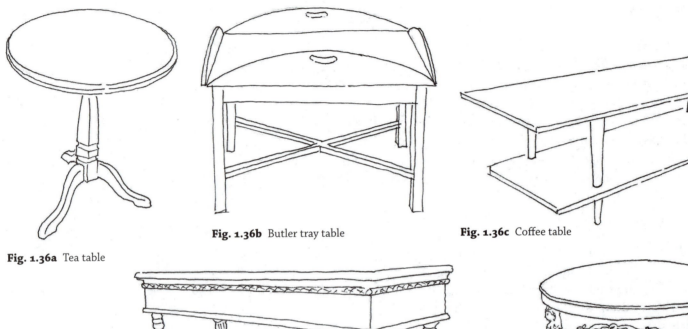

Fig. 1.36b Butler tray table

Fig. 1.36c Coffee table

Fig. 1.36a Tea table

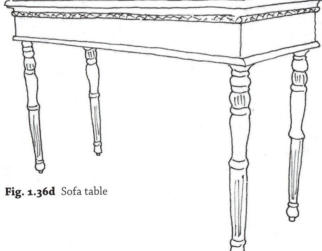

Fig. 1.36d Sofa table

Fig. 1.36e Side table—Empire

Bedroom Furniture

Bedroom furniture starts with the bed itself. The bed can be designed in many different styles, and its size is designed around the mattress size. (See Figures 1.37a through f.) The rest of the pieces in the bedroom are typically designed for storage and match the style of the bed. (See Figure 1.38.)

Fig. 1.37a Four-poster bed

Fig. 1.37b Canopy bed

Fig. 1.37c Sleigh bed

Fig. 1.37d Bunk bed—Mission

Fig. 1.37e Day bed

Fig. 1.37f Trundle—Traditional

Fig. 1.38 Blanket chest

Chapter 1 Project and Quiz

Project

Directions: Sketch different styles of furniture:

1. Create 10 sketches of different styles of furniture, one per page.
2. Create one detail for each piece on the same page.
3. Label each sketch with the style, year, and a brief description of the piece. Shade images in with pencil to create the volume of the piece. For example:

Chippendale, 1750–1790,
Lowboy with detail of the claw foot

Quiz

PART 1

Directions: Put these furniture styles in chronological order.

1. _____ Queen Anne
2. _____ Art Deco
3. _____ Empire
4. _____ Jacobean
5. _____ Victorian

PART 2

Directions: Match the style with its definition below.

6. Federal _____
7. Biedermeier _____
8. Arts and Crafts _____
9. Pennsylvania Dutch _____
10. Shaker _____

A. Many of these pieces feature light to dark brown stains or colorful folk painting.
B. This German style of furniture has curved lines and contrasting features.
C. Common details are tapered legs, ladder-back chairs, and simple wooden knobs.
D. This furniture style combines both Hepplewhite and Sheraton.
E. This style is also known as Mission style.

The Design Process

THIS CHAPTER WILL show the design process as it relates to furniture design, following the Council for Interior Design Accreditation (CIDA) design process guidelines that include the following:

- **Programming:** Understanding the client's needs and problem identification.
- **Schematics:** Creating quick sketches and developing rough ideas.
- **Design Development:** Drafting images in scale, drawing in perspective, and marker-rendering finish materials.
- **Contract Administration:** Contract documents and detailing of the furniture design

▸ **Evaluation:** Understanding the function, durability, and the end user.

This chapter begins with a discussion about how human ergonomics dictates the dimensions of different pieces of furniture; examples are shown. Then follows a step-by-step process for creating simple sketches, drafts, perspective, and finished marker renderings with example illustrations of each stage.

Human Ergonomics

There are many different ways to design a piece of furniture. This book views furniture as a piece of functional sculpture. To be fully functional, the piece must relate to basic human ergonomics. Ergonomics is the science of designing objects for human use by maximizing efficiency and quality.

For example, the work surface height of a dining table or kitchen nook table should be 29 to 30 inches (see Figure 2.1a). This dimension is based on the height of a person seated in a dining chair. The seat height of the dining chair is based on the popliteal height, which is the dimension from the floor to the height behind the knee. That dimension ranges from 17 to 19 inches for adults. These

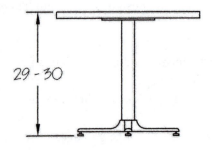

TABLE HEIGHT (floor to top of work surface)

Fig. 2.1a The work surface height of a dining table or kitchen nook table should be 29″ to 30″.

particular measurements are necessary because of human ergonomics and because of the way one object affects another. The size of the table is based on having 24 inches of minimum space for the seated person and 8 inches of space on each side, although 30 inches of space for the seated person and 12 inches on each side is preferred (see Figure 2.1b). The 24 inches of minimum space for the seated person and the preferred 30 inches is the same for a rectangular table (see Figure 2.1c). Circular tables have different issues when it comes to spacing because a person seated at a circular table has a pie-shaped space on the surface of the table, thus necessitating a larger diameter table compared to a square or rectangular table because the space in the center of the table is difficult to access (see Figure 2.1d).

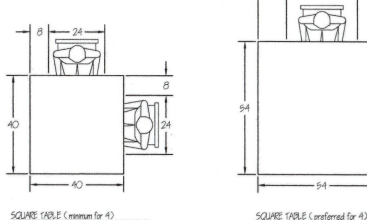

SQUARE TABLE (minimum for 4)

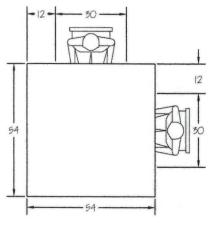

SQUARE TABLE (preferred for 4)

Fig. 2.1b The size of the table is based on having 24″ of minimum space for the seated person and 8″ of space on each side, but 30″ and 12″, respectively, are preferred.

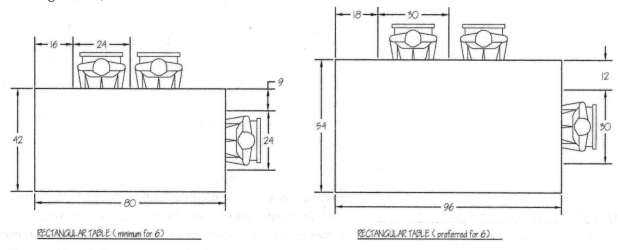

RECTANGULAR TABLE (minimum for 6)

RECTANGULAR TABLE (preferred for 6)

Fig. 2.1c The 24″ of minimum space for the seated person and a preferred 30″ is the same for a rectangular table.

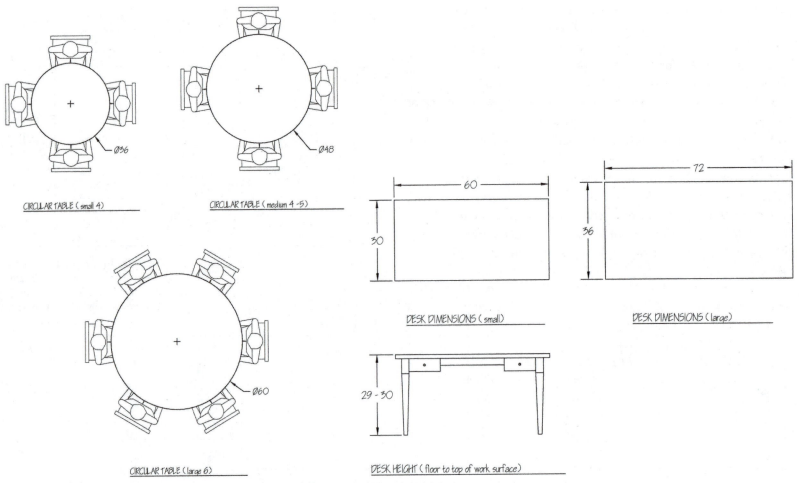

CIRCULAR TABLE (small 4)

CIRCULAR TABLE (medium 4 -5)

Ø36

Ø48

CIRCULAR TABLE (large 6)

Ø60

DESK DIMENSIONS (small)

60

30

DESK DIMENSIONS (large)

72

36

DESK HEIGHT (floor to top of work surface)

29 - 30

Fig. 2.1d Circular table with a pie shape of space on the table surface and hard-to-access space in the center of the table.

Fig. 2.1e A desk's height is similar to that of a table.

Similar to tables, the height of a desk should be 29 to 30 inches. One main consideration when designing a desk is the armchair that will be used with it. The height of the armrest needs to be lower than the bottom of the top drawer; a basic rule is to have at least ¾ inch of clearance. The plan view dimensions of a desk can vary; Figure 2.1e shows two basic sizes for a desk. (Plan views are discussed later in this chapter, in the section "Drafting in Orthographic Projection.")

Beds are designed based on standard mattress sizes. These sizes range from crib (28″ × 52″), twin (39″ × 75″), full (54″ × 75″), queen (60″ × 80″), king (76″ × 80″) up to the largest mattress, the California king (72″ × 84″). The dimensions of standard mattress sizes include length, which is based on the height of a person, and width, which is designed for either one or two persons. (See Figure 2.2.) The depth depends on the manufacturer; typically, a mattress comes with a box spring that adds to the overall depth. The box spring is an upholstered frame, on top of which the mattress is positioned and which fits between the bed's rails, footboard, and headboard. The total height from the floor to the top of the mattress ranges from 20 to 30 inches.

A common mistake with students' drawings is incorrect proportions, such as making the tabletop height too tall. One way to start visualizing dimensions of an object's work surface height, for example, a dining table, is to base the proportion on something you might already know that is standardized, such as cabinetry. Kitchen cabinets

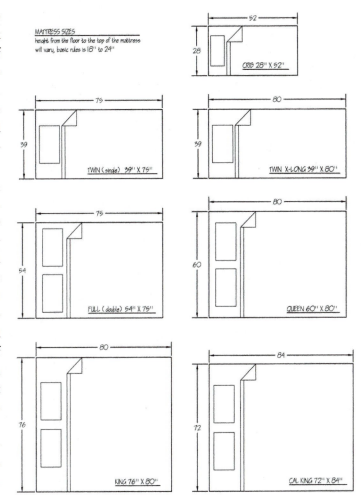

Fig. 2.2 Mattress sizes.

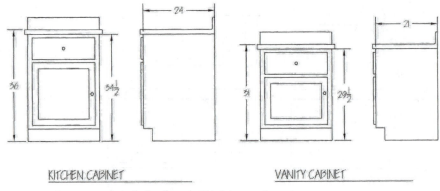

Fig. 2.3 Elevation views of a kitchen and bathroom cabinet.

are 36 inches in height, and bathroom cabinets are 31 to 36 inches. A dining table height is 29 to 30 inches. When you start to sketch, visualizing the object's space will help to develop the correct proportions. The drawing in Figure 2.3 shows the dimensions of a kitchen cabinet and a bathroom vanity cabinet.

Programming

The design process starts with programming, which means understanding the client's needs and identifying any possible problems. The first step is to listen to clients and decipher their ideas, wants, or needs. This is also the part of the process during which the designer can brainstorm ideas with the client so that everyone is on the same page from the beginning. Sometimes clients may be vague in what they want or they may have so many ideas and styles that the designer will need to edit the ideas into a clear vision.

Schematics: Sketching

The schematic part of the process is about developing rough ideas by creating quick thumbnail sketches in front of the client so that the designer and the client can start to visualize the ideas. Other sketching can be done to develop ideas further by adjusting the proportions of elements and dimensions.

Sketching is a quick way to create and modify ideas. Using a pencil, you can create light lines showing the basic shape of a piece—top, legs, drawers, and so on. Then you can draw on top of the sketch with a darker line while altering the proportions and dimensions to change the look of the piece. These initial sketches should be quick and loose thumbnail gestures, about 3 to 4 inches tall and wide, created without worry about erasing mistakes. To change the design, create another thumbnail sketch. Designers often sketch between 20 and 30 thumbnails to create a design. These sketches each take about 30 seconds to a minute. The advantage of creating multiple thumbnails is that you can often see parts in different sketches that you can combine for the final thumbnail. The thumbnails in Figure 2.4a show how quickly an idea can develop, simply by using a style as an influence. The first image shows a geometric base created by drawing through the object to help keep it round, then changing how those parts are arranged for the other designs.

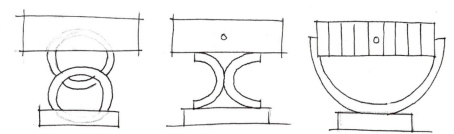

Fig. 2.4a Nightstand with an Art Deco influence.

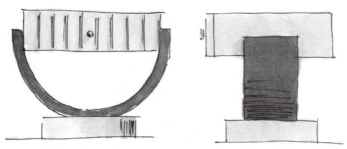

Fig. 2.4b The front and side views of the nightstand.

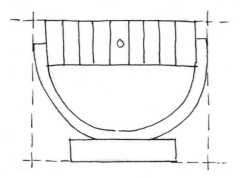

Fig. 2.5 Hand sketch of a nightstand in elevation view.

Sketching the side view helps to show the proportions of the object. The image in Figure 2.4b was marker-rendered with basic tones. Using basic tones can be an important part of the sketch when contrasting materials or colors need to be shown. You do not need to show detail to get your point across to a client or builder. Figure 2.4b took about 5 minutes to complete.

Sometimes a client may have difficulty seeing a three-dimensional object like furniture as a flat sketch and will need to see the volume of the piece. This can be done fairly easily by creating the full volume of the object and then subtracting the space. Figure 2.5 shows a thumbnail sketch with a dotted square around it. That square is the total volume that the three-dimensional object will start with. Figures 2.6a to f start with a transparent cube sketched in 2-point perspective and then use the proportions of the cube to add the detail of the object. The final three-dimensional sketch is marker-rendered with basic tones. It is still a quick drawing—this object took about 5 to 7 minutes to completely render.

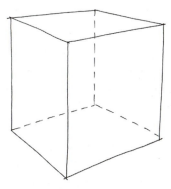

Fig. 2.6a The total volume sketched as a transparent cube.

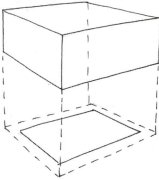

Fig. 2.6b The basic proportions of the top and base are drawn. Note the base is drawn as the footprint first because it's a smaller item and doses not extend to the edges.

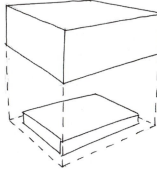

Fig. 2.6c Vertical dimension is added to the footprint.

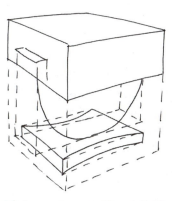

Fig. 2.6d A curve is created by subdividing the base in a rectilinear fashion by bringing the vertical dashed lines down from the sides and across the base. This creates a start, middle, and end for the curve, and it will give the curve the correct proportions.

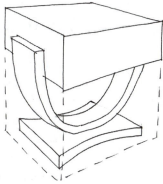

Fig. 2.6e The rest of the curves are drawn based off the original curve to show the thickness of those materials.

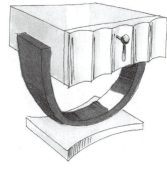

Fig. 2.6f Final three-dimensional sketch with detail added.

Design Development

Once the sketching is done it is time to develop the idea into a measured drawing, either by manually drafting the image or by using the computer. This will verify the proportions of the piece, and by drafting the piece in scale it will be possible to ensure that items such as a television will fit into the piece. At this point, the designer can also recreate the piece in a perspective in order to show it in three dimensions as well as creating marker renderings to show the finish materials and tones.

Drafting

Drafting is a great way to transform a thumbnail sketch into a measured working drawing. This is where you may need to adjust your proportions based on human ergonomics and how they may affect the piece. A basic architectural scale ruler is all you need to draw the piece with the exact proportions of the piece that will be built.

Understanding an architectural scale ruler is simple. The ruler creates a scale factor depending on which side of the ruler you use. This gives you the ability to draft an image with exact proportions and dimensions. The ruler measures feet on one side and up to 12 inches on the other. The scale factor is given by a number in the top corner.

Furniture typically is drawn in ¾-inch or 1-inch scale. Details can be created in larger drawings such as in 3-inch scale. (See Figures 2.7a through c.)

Overseas furniture manufacturers use the metric system. Metric scale rulers are completely different from the architectural scale, which uses a scale factor of 1 inch equals 1 foot, 0 inches and uses feet and inches as its measuring unit. The metric scale uses a ratio such as 1:20, which means that the item being drawn is 20 times smaller than the actual item. The metric system breaks down the meter (m) into equal parts of ten, or decimeters (dm). The decimeter is divided into equal parts of ten, or centimeters (cm). The centimeter is divided into equal parts of ten, or millimeters (mm). The best way for students who are not used to the metric system to understand this is to see a meter stick to visualize that there are 100cm or 1,000mm in a meter.

AutoCAD (a program that allows computer-aided design) can speed up the design process. It is a great tool for creating working drawings and making changes to drawings, but it is just a tool, like a pencil and ruler. Three main questions about using AutoCAD when designing furniture are:

► **What scale to print at?** The scale should be a ¾- to 1-inch scale, and details can be created in view ports at 3-inch scale. The important thing is that the scale is large enough to clearly see what is going on in the detail.

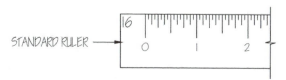

Fig. 2.7a Standard ruler.

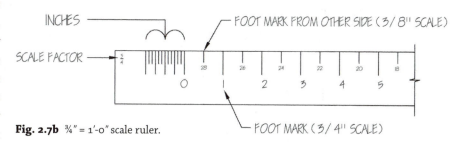

Fig. 2.7b ¾″ = 1′-0″ scale ruler.

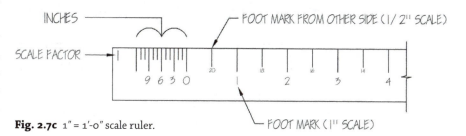

Fig. 2.7c 1″ = 1′-0″ scale ruler.

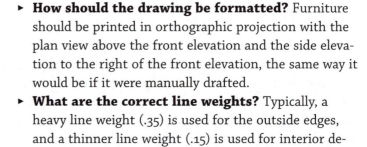

▸ **How should the drawing be formatted?** Furniture should be printed in orthographic projection with the plan view above the front elevation and the side elevation to the right of the front elevation, the same way it would be if it were manually drafted.

▸ **What are the correct line weights?** Typically, a heavy line weight (.35) is used for the outside edges, and a thinner line weight (.15) is used for interior details such as drawers and doors. Hidden line weights should also be thinner (.13 or .09).

AutoCAD also comes in different versions and is updated each year. The year is added to the name of the program, for example, AutoCAD2008. If you do not plan on drawing in three dimensions, a light version, or LT, is available: AutoCAD2008LT.

Drafting in Orthographic Projection

Orthographic projection involves drafting a three-dimensional object like furniture in at least three flat views. These views are plan view (top view), front elevation (front view), and side elevation (side view). The basic format for an orthographic projection is a plan view that lines up above the front elevation, and a side elevation that lines up to the side of the front elevation. (See Figure 2.8.)

Other views that can be shown are detail views and section views. Detail views are created when the orthographic

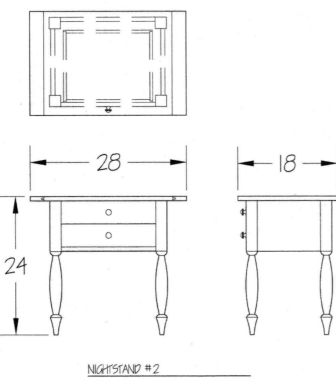

NIGHTSTAND #2

Fig. 2.8 Example of AutoCAD orthographic projection.

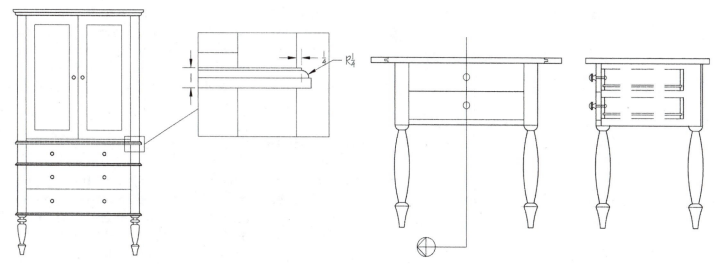

Fig. 2.9a Example of an armoire detail.

Fig. 2.9b Example of a section drawing.

drawing does not show small details like edge or molding. If needed, a larger scaled image is created to show the thickness of materials or a profile of an edge detail, for example. A section view is the drawing that represents the inside construction of the piece. In other words, the view is as if someone cut the piece in half, showing the inside details. (See Figures 2.9a and 2.9b.)

One final important note about drafting is that you can show the dimensions of the piece of furniture and its parts. This can give a clear idea of how large that piece will be and helps to explain your design intent and protect the integrity of the design from misunderstandings during the

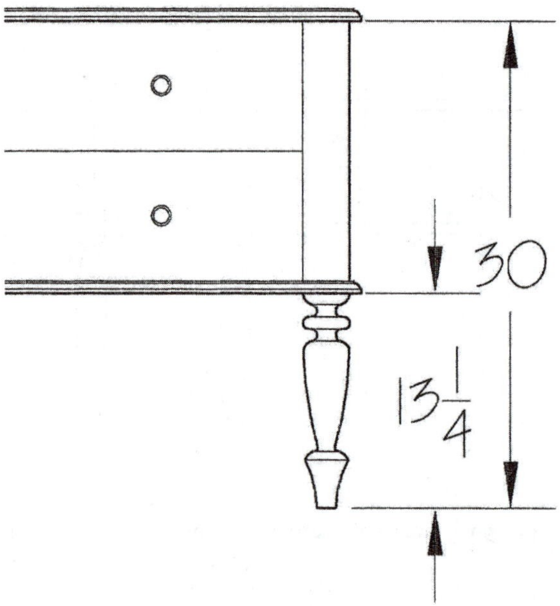

Fig. 2.10 Example of dimensioning.

fabrication process. From there you can create a parts list that will speed up the construction process. The dimensions of furniture typically are shown in inches (rather than feet and inches), like the example in Figure 2.10 showing the leg at 30 inches instead of 2 feet, 6 inches.

Isometric Drawing

An isometric drawing shows an object in three dimensions. This drawing can be measured and drawn from the orthographic projection. All the dimensions of the piece will be the same in both the orthographic and isometric drawings. Each side of the object will be drawn at 30 degrees, which will show the front, side, and top of the piece. The vertical lines of the object will still be drawn vertically, but the rest will be drawn at a 30-degree angle. (See Figures 2.11a through c.)

Perspective Drawing

Perspective displays an object as a three-dimensional drawing in the same way the eye sees it in three-dimensional space. This means that the three-dimensional piece will have a vanishing point when it is drawn. There are three basic types of perspective drawings: 1-point, 2-point, and 3-point perspective. The type of perspective drawing is based on how many vanishing points there are in the

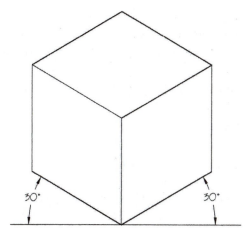

Fig. 2.11a Example of a cube drawn in isometric view.

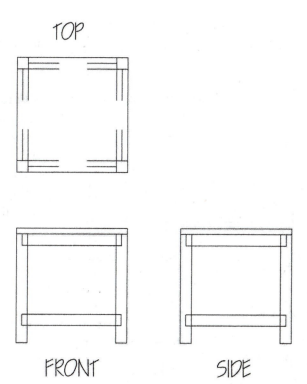

TOP

FRONT   SIDE

Fig. 2.11b An orthographic projection of a simple square stool.

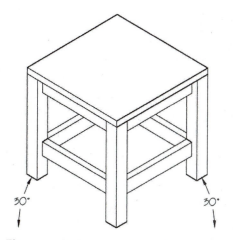

Fig. 2.11c That same stool in isometric view.

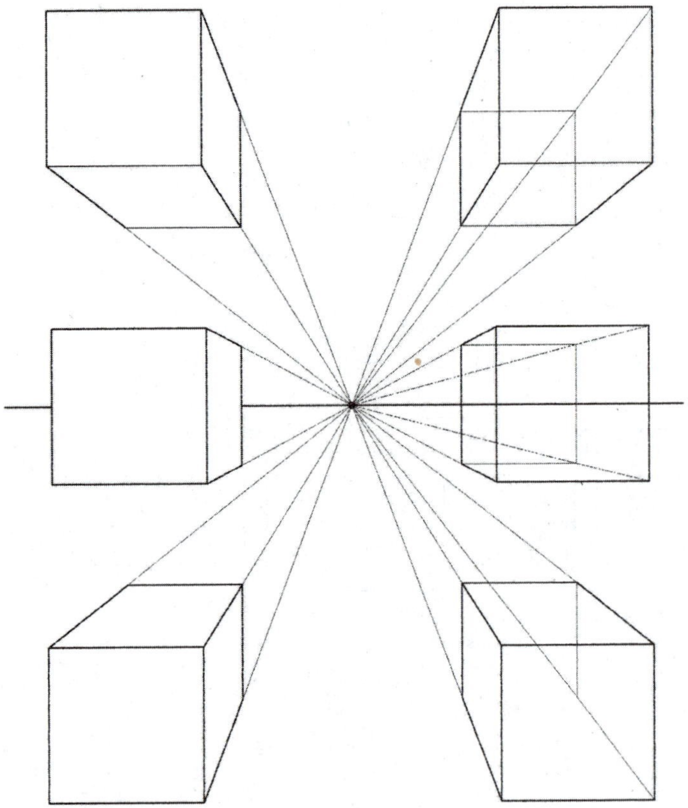

drawing. The vanishing point is based on how the object is positioned. When drawing furniture, you should typically use 1-point or 2-point perspective:

▸ **1-Point Perspective:** This view provides one vanishing point to the object. Therefore, the front of the object will appear straight-on to the viewer. (See Figure 2.12.)
▸ **2-Point Perspective:** This view provides two vanishing points to the object because the object is now turned at an angle to the viewer. (See Figure 2.13.)

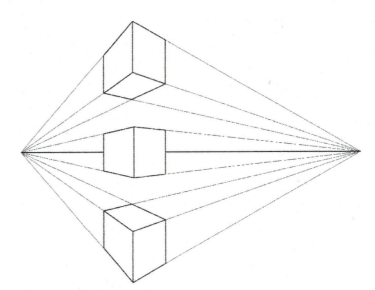

Fig. 2.12 Example showing solid cubes above, below, and on the horizon line.

Fig. 2.13 Example showing solid cubes above, below, and on the horizon line.

Each perspective has basic rules, and once you under-stand these rules you will be able to draw anything three-dimensionally:

- ▸ **Rule 1:** The horizon line represents the viewer's eye level.
- ▸ **Rule 2:** The vanishing point or points will be placed on that horizon line.
- ▸ **Rule 3:** Surface planes that go from the front of an object to the back will be represented as a line in a per-spective that starts at the front and lines up with the vanishing point.

Eye level refers to how high or low the horizon line is placed on the drawing. The higher the horizon line, the higher the eye level of the viewer. The three images in Fig-ures 2.14a through c show how the object changes when the eye level changes.

Creating Shadows in Perspective

Figure 2.15 shows the step-by-step process for creating a shadow for a cube in 2-point perspective. This is the paral-lel method. Starting with a transparent cube, draw a line at the front bottom corner, then repeat to the bottom side and back corners drawing parallel lines, as shown in step 2. Draw an angled line down from the front top corner to the first ground shadow line. This angle will make the

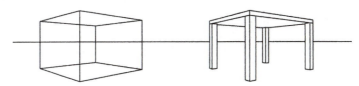

Fig. 2.14a The horizon line at a child's eye level.

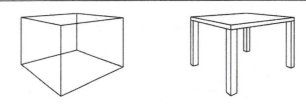

Fig. 2.14b The eye level now at an adult seating level.

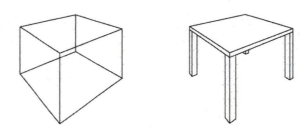

Fig. 2.14c The eye level now at adult standing level.

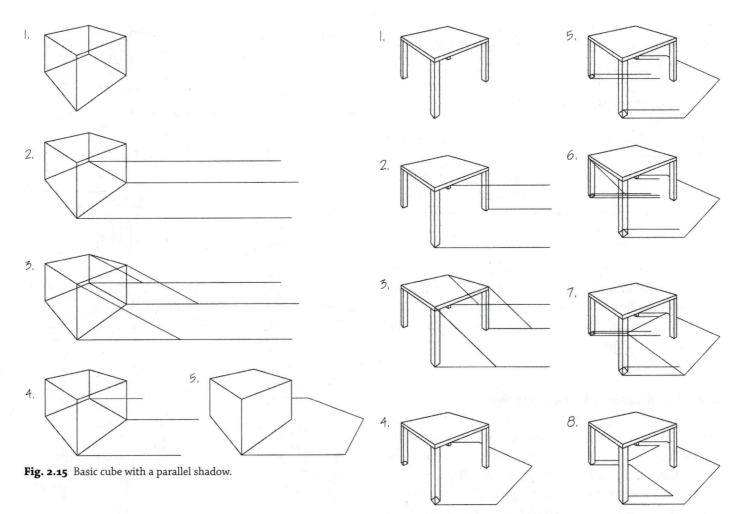

Fig. 2.15 Basic cube with a parallel shadow.

Fig. 2.16 Basic table with a parallel shadow.

shadow shorter or longer depending on the angle. Repeat with the other top corners creating angled lines parallel to the first angled line, as shown in step 3. Where these lines cross, the end of the shadow is created. Erase and connect the end to create the complete shadow, as shown in steps 4 and 5.

Creating a shadow for a piece of furniture looks difficult but is actually quite simple. (See Figure 2.16.) Steps 1 through 4 are the same as the cube. Treat the piece as a solid object without detail to create the outside of the shadow. For detail follow the steps shown. Step 5 shows lines parallel to step 2. Step 6 is an angled line parallel to the line in step 3. Then connect the lines as shown in step 7; this is where the edges of the top meet the end of the center leg. Erase the lines inside the shadow outline, and the shadow is now complete.

Marker-Rendering

The basic reason to use markers is to replicate the finished look of the piece. Markers may take some time to get used to, but they are a fast way to show clients what they are buying before the construction starts. With markers, the designer and client can both understand what the piece will look like when completed.

Treat the rendering as a quick sketch. Start with colors that are lighter than the material that you are trying to recreate, as in Figure 2.17. Creating a light source will add

Fig. 2.17 Example of a hand sketch that has been rendered with technical pen, Dark Brown, French Grey 60% with Cloud Blue for the background.

to the dimension of the piece. You can do this by using grey-tone markers to add shadow effects. Other effects can be created with color pencil, such as adding wood grain on top of the marker, and highlights can be created with white pencil or Wite-Out.

Contract Administration

In this part of the process the designer documents the piece of furniture while explaining the dimensions, materials finish, details of the piece, and expected time of completion. This documentation, along with drawings, is sent to the custom builder or builders for bids on the fabrication of the piece. That cost of construction is then added to the documentation so that it can be sent to the client for approval before the construction begins. Some custom furniture builders will not deliver the piece to the client; in that case a delivery company needs to be hired, and that cost must be added to the contract.

Evaluation

The evaluation process is the last stage before the client takes possession of the piece. The designer should inspect the final piece to make sure that it was built according to the contract. The designer also must ensure that it functions the way it was designed as well as checking that the finish matches the sample. It is a good idea for the designer to see the piece when fabrication is done and before the finish is applied. It is easier and quicker to fix any problems and keep the project on schedule at this point rather than waiting until the end.

Chapter 2 Project and Quiz

Project: The design process as it relates to furniture.

PART 1: SKETCHES

Directions: Create 20 thumbnail sketches of furniture, using historic influences for some of the sketches. These 20 thumbnail sketches should be in pencil and should fit on one or two sheets of paper. They can evolve from one drawing into another and be simple front and side views.

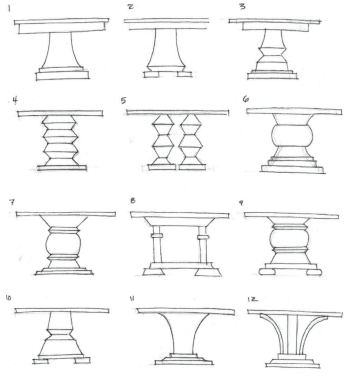

Fig. 2.18 Example of thumbnail sketches.

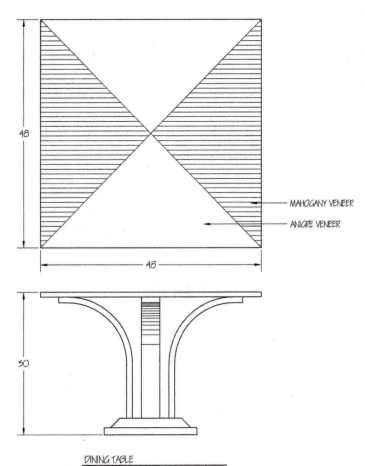

Fig. 2.19 Example of drafted orthographic drawing.

MAHOGANY VENEER

ANIGRE VENEER

48

48

30

DINING TABLE

SCALE - 1" = 1'-0"

PART 2: ORTHOGRAPHIC PROJECTION

Directions: Create a drafted orthographic drawing of one thumbnail idea; make sure it is ergonomically correct and drawn at scale 1 inch equals 1 foot, 0 inches or ¾ inch equals 1 foot, 0 inches.

PART 3: PERSPECTIVE SKETCH

Directions: Create a 2-point perspective sketch of the piece; add tones with technical pen or markers.

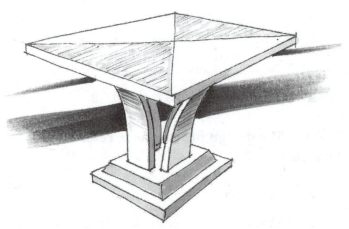

Fig. 2.20 Example of 2-point perspective sketch.

Quiz

Directions: Circle the best answer choice for each of the following questions.

1. What is the height of a dining table work surface?
    A. 24″   B. 30″   C. 32″

2. What is the minimum space needed for someone seated at a dining table?
    A. 18″   B. 24″   C. 30″

3. What is the size of a twin mattress?
    A. 30″ × 75″   B. 36″ × 80″   C. 39″ × 75″

4. What is the size of a queen mattress?
    A. 54″ × 75″   B. 60″ × 75″   C. 60″ × 80″

5. What is the size of a king mattress?
    A. 70″ × 80″   B. 76″ × 80″   C. 72″ × 84″

6. What is the size of a California king mattress?
    A. 70″ × 80″   B. 76″ × 80″   C. 72″ × 84″

7. What is an orthographic projection drawing?
    A. a side cutaway view
    B. a three-dimensional drawing
    C. a drawing that shows top, front, and side

8. What is an isometric drawing?
    A. three flat images
    B. a drawing with a horizon line
    C. a drawing that can be measured

9. Which view is the plan view of an image?
    A. front B. side C. top

10. What does a section view show?
    A. cutaway interior view
    B. top view of a piece
    C. side view of a piece

CHAPTER 3

Materials: Woods and Metals

THIS CHAPTER DEFINES the different types of materials used for furniture design and construction. It shows how hardwood and softwood lumber, as well as man-made materials, are sold and also discusses the basic dimensions of materials such as plywood, medium-density fiberboard (MDF), and veneers. The last part of this chapter describes different types of metals and the construction methods for those metals.

Hardwoods and Softwoods

Wood can be categorized into two different groups: hardwoods and softwoods. You might naturally think that the difference between these two types of woods is that one is hard and one is soft; however, this is not the case. In fact, the difference is based on the tree's greenery. Hardwood trees like maple, oak, and walnut have leaves, whereas softwood trees like cedar, Douglas fir, and pine have needles. Hard versus soft has nothing to do with the strength of the wood; for example, balsa wood is a soft, light wood that is used in model building, yet it is categorized as a hardwood because it comes from a tree with leaves.

Most of the time a wood is chosen for its figure, which refers to the color, grain, and appearance of the wood. For example, maple is available in many types. Hard maple will have a blond, yellow color and medium grain. Bird's-eye maple will have those features as well as a raised dotted appearance to the flat surface. The figure is what makes a material unique. To appreciate the true figure of the wood, it needs to be seen in person because an image will not show the depth of the material. In some cases, a wood is used because of its natural characteristics such as teak for outdoor furniture. Teak has natural oils in the wood fibers that protect it from the elements better than any other type of wood. Another reason that one wood may be chosen over another is its cost—for example, when used for a piece of furniture that will be painted. Poplar is a low-cost wood with a fine grain that takes paint well.

Box 3.1 lists typical hardwoods and the area of the world where they grow.

Box 3.1

Typical Hardwoods and Their Origins

NORTH AMERICAN WOODS

Alder	Hickory	Maple Soft
Ash	Maple Bird's-Eye	Oak Red
Birch	Maple Curly	Oak White
Cherry	Maple Hard	Poplar
Cypress	Maple Quilted	Walnut Black

CENTRAL AND SOUTH AMERICAN WOODS

Bloodwood	Mahogany Genuine	Rosewood Brazilian
Cocobolo	Monkey Pod	Tulipwood
Jatoba/	Purple Heart	Walnut Tropical
Brazilian Cherry	Leopardwood	

AFRICAN WOODS

Anigre	Ebony	Wengé
Bubinga	Mahogany African	Zebrawood
	Padauk	

ASIAN AND THE SOUTH PACIFIC ISLAND WOODS

Ebony Macassar	Eucalyptus Figured	Teak
	Rosewood	

EUROPEAN WOODS

Beech	English Brown Oak	Walnut English

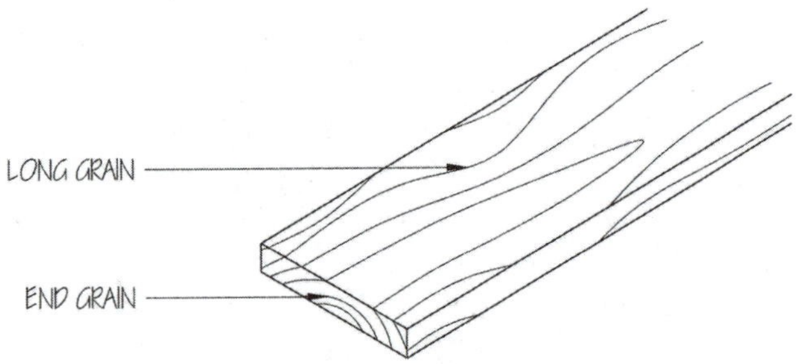

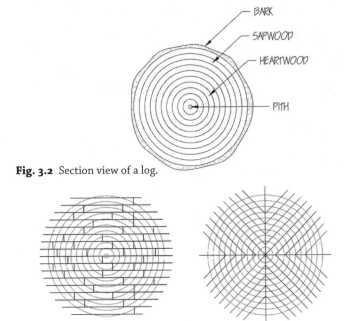

Fig. 3.1 The difference between end and long grain.

Fig. 3.2 Section view of a log.

Fig. 3.3 The difference between typical cut and quartersawn lumber.

These solid wood boards have a long grain, which is the direction of the wood, and an end grain, which is the end of the board. The end grain shows the growth rings of the tree. Figure 3.1 shows the difference between the long and end grains.

A log can be broken down into four basic parts (see Figure 3.2):

▸ **Pith:** Center of the material
▸ **Heartwood:** Structural part of the trunk
▸ **Sapwood:** Part of the trunk that transports nutrients through the tree
▸ **Bark:** Outer protective layer

Once the bark is peeled from the log, it then can be cut in a number of different ways, depending on the species. Two popular methods are quartersawn and through-and-through cut or plain sawn, as shown in Figure 3.3.

Quartersawn lumber costs more than typical cut lumber for two reasons. First, there is more wasted lumber with quartersawn wood. Second, the growth rings run straight across the board, which makes quartersawn lumber more stable and less likely to warp than through-and-through cut.

At the lumberyard, wood materials are separated by species and thickness. The thickness is a rough-cut dimension and will be planed down by the furniture builder to finished thickness, which is shown in Table 3.1 as normal

Table 3.1

Actual and Normal Sizes

Quarters	Actual Size	Normal Size
4/4	1″	¾″
5/4	1¼″	1″
6/4	1½″	1¼″
7/4	1¾″	1½″
8/4	2″	1¾″
9/4	2¼″	2″
10/4	2½″	2¼″

size. The thickness is based on quarters of material starting with 4 quarter or 4/4, which is 1-inch thick.

Hardwood and softwood lumber is sold by the board foot (bf). One board foot has dimensions of 12-inches by 12-inches by 1-inch thick. This measuring system is used because the lumber will be cut based on the size of each particular log. These logs will come from the trunk of the tree, not from branch material, because of the structural nature of the trunk. This means that the boards may vary in width and length depending on the size of each tree's trunk; a board that is 6 inches wide, 1 inch thick, and 8 feet long is configured as 4 board feet (4bf). Each type of wood will be priced per board foot, and just like any commodity, the price changes from season to season. The following three tables provide a handy reference for board feet. For example, you can use Table 3.2 to see that a 4/4 board that is 10 inches long and 4 inches wide is a total of 3.33 board feet. (See Table 3.3 and Table 3.4.)

Table 3.2

4/4 Thick Board Foot: Double for 8/4 Thickness

	1″	2″	3″	4″	5″	6″	7″	8″	9″	10″	11″	12″
1′	0.08	0.16	0.25	0.33	0.41	0.5	0.58	0.66	0.75	0.83	0.91	1
2′	0.17	0.33	0.50	0.66	0.83	1.0	1.16	1.33	1.50	1.66	1.83	2
3′	0.25	0.50	0.75	1.00	1.25	1.5	1.75	2.00	2.25	2.50	2.75	3
4′	0.33	0.66	1.00	1.33	1.66	2.0	2.33	2.66	3.00	3.33	3.66	4
5′	0.41	0.83	1.25	1.66	2.08	2.5	2.91	3.33	3.75	4.16	4.58	5
6′	0.50	1.00	1.50	2.00	2.50	3.0	3.50	4.00	4.50	5.00	5.50	6
7′	0.58	1.16	1.75	2.33	2.91	3.5	4.08	4.66	5.25	5.83	6.41	7
8′	0.66	1.33	2.00	2.66	3.33	4.0	4.66	5.33	6.00	6.66	7.33	8
9′	0.75	1.50	2.25	3.00	3.75	4.5	5.25	6.00	6.75	7.50	8.25	9
10′	0.83	1.66	2.50	3.33	4.16	5.0	5.83	6.66	7.50	8.33	9.16	10
11′	0.91	1.83	2.75	3.66	4.58	5.5	6.41	7.33	8.25	9.16	10.08	11
12′	1.00	2.00	3.00	4.00	5.00	6.0	7.00	8.00	9.00	10.00	11.00	12

Table 3.3
5/4 Thick Board Foot:
Double for 10/4 Thickness

	1"	2"	3"	4"	5"	6"	7"	8"	9"	10"	11"	12"
1'	0.10	0.20	0.31	0.41	0.52	0.62	0.72	0.83	0.93	1.04	1.14	1.25
2'	0.20	0.41	0.62	0.83	1.04	1.25	1.45	1.66	1.87	2.08	2.29	2.50
3'	0.31	0.62	0.93	1.25	1.58	1.87	2.18	2.50	2.81	3.12	3.43	3.75
4'	0.41	0.83	1.25	1.66	2.08	2.50	2.91	3.33	3.75	4.16	4.58	5.00
5'	0.52	1.04	1.56	2.08	2.60	3.12	3.64	4.16	4.68	5.20	5.72	6.25
6'	0.62	1.25	1.87	2.50	3.12	3.75	4.37	5.00	5.62	6.25	6.87	7.50
7'	0.72	1.45	2.18	2.91	3.64	4.37	5.10	5.83	6.56	7.29	8.02	8.75
8'	0.83	1.66	2.50	3.33	4.16	5.00	5.83	6.66	7.50	8.33	9.16	10.00
9'	0.93	1.87	2.81	3.75	4.68	5.62	6.56	7.50	8.43	9.37	10.31	11.25
10'	1.04	2.08	3.12	4.16	5.20	6.25	7.29	8.33	9.37	10.41	11.45	12.50
11'	1.14	2.29	3.43	4.58	5.72	6.87	8.02	9.16	10.31	11.45	12.60	13.75
12'	1.25	2.50	3.75	5.00	6.25	7.50	8.75	10.00	11.25	12.50	13.75	15.00

Table 3.4
6/4 Thick Board Foot:
Double for 12/4 Thickness

	1"	2"	3"	4"	5"	6"	7"	8"	9"	10"	11"	12"
1'	0.12	0.25	0.37	0.5	0.62	0.75	0.87	1	1.12	1.25	1.37	1.5
2'	0.25	0.50	0.75	1.0	1.25	1.50	1.75	2	2.25	2.50	2.75	3.0
3'	0.37	0.75	1.12	1.5	1.87	2.25	2.62	3	3.37	3.75	4.12	4.5
4'	0.50	1.00	1.50	2.0	2.50	3.00	3.50	4	4.50	5.00	5.50	6.0
5'	0.62	1.25	1.87	2.5	3.12	3.75	4.37	5	5.62	6.25	6.87	7.5
6'	0.75	1.50	2.25	3.0	3.75	4.50	5.25	6	6.75	7.50	8.25	9.0
7'	0.87	1.75	2.62	3.5	4.37	5.25	6.12	7	7.87	8.75	9.62	10.5
8'	1.00	2.00	3.00	4.0	5.00	6.00	7.00	8	9.00	10.00	11.00	12.0
9'	1.12	2.25	3.37	4.5	5.62	6.75	7.87	9	10.12	11.25	12.37	13.5
10'	1.25	2.50	3.75	5.0	6.25	7.50	8.75	10	11.25	12.50	13.75	15.0
11'	1.37	2.75	4.12	5.5	6.87	8.25	9.62	11	12.37	13.75	15.12	16.2
12'	1.50	3.00	4.50	6.0	7.50	9.00	10.50	12	13.50	15.00	16.50	18.0

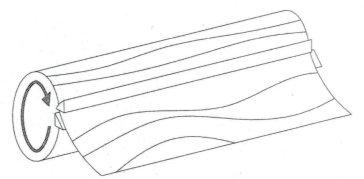

Fig. 3.4a Material being peeled to create rotary cut veneer.

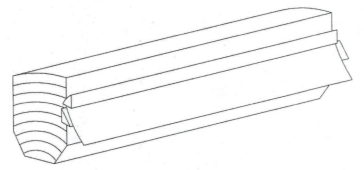

Fig. 3.4b Material being peeled to create quartersawn cut veneer.

Veneers

Veneers are created by peeling or slicing material off a log to produce a thin sheet of wood. (See Figures 3.4a and 3.4b.) They typically are available in sizes of 4 feet by 8 feet and 2 feet by 8 feet in any species of wood. In some cases, the veneer is pieced together because small-diameter trees produce small widths of veneers. These smaller widths are then glued together to a paper backing to create the standard sheet sizes. Veneers also come in 10-millimeter paper-backed or 22-millimeter-thick sizes. The difference between the two is that the 22 millimeter veneer is just the wood veneer itself, whereas the paper-backed veneer has paper glued to the back of the veneer, which uses a thinner veneer material. The thinner veneer with the paper backing lends itself to curved surfaces better than the thicker 22 millimeter veneer.

Veneers are applied in two different ways. The first way uses contact cement that is applied to the back of the veneer and the surface that it will be glued to. The contact cement dries so that when the veneer is attached to the surface it instantly bonds. The second way uses a vacuum press. In this method, special glue is applied to the back of the veneer as well as to the surface that it will be glued to. Then both pieces are placed in a vacuum bag, and a vacuum compressor pulls the air out of the bag, creating pressure on the overall surface and bonding the veneer in 2 to 4 hours after the glue dries.

Plywoods

Plywoods are man-made products used for many different applications. Plywood is basically thin panels of wood that are peeled off the log and then glued together in alternating layers or plies. The wood direction of each ply runs perpendicular to the next, thus preventing warping and giving the plywood strength. (See Figure 3.5.) Plywood is constructed with an odd number of plies to prevent the plywood from warping. Higher grades of plywood have a higher number of plies, thus adding to the stability of the material. Standard construction-grade plywood has three plies, whereas furniture-grade plywood starts at five plies. These plies are typically made from Douglas fir with an outer veneer layer of finished material such as maple. This veneer layer is almost paper thin and is applied at the factory on both sides of the wood. (See Figure 3.6.) Therefore, the edge of the plywood will show the core material or plies of wood.

Dimensions of Plywood

The main design limitation of plywood is designing around the production sizes available. Plywood for furniture application typically is available in three standard thicknesses: ¼ inch, ½ inch, and ¾ inch. For special applications other sizes are available including ⅜-inch, ⅝-inch, and 1-inch thicknesses.

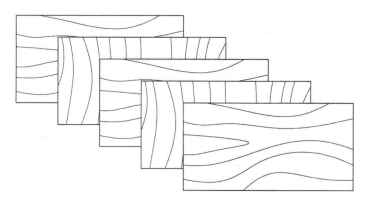

Fig. 3.5 Direction of wood grain for each ply before factory has glued them together.

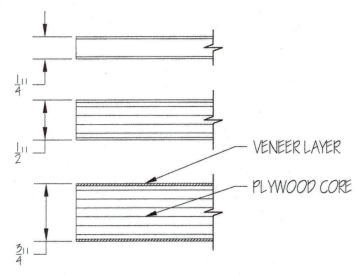

VENEER LAYER

PLYWOOD CORE

Fig. 3.6 Edge detail of plywood.

- ▸ ¼-inch material is used for the backs of cabinets and the bottoms of drawers.
- ▸ ½-inch material is used mainly for drawer box construction.
- ▸ ¾-inch material is used for the structural parts of furniture, walls, shelves, and floors.

The overall dimensions of plywood are typically 48 inches by 96 inches, or what is commonly known as 4 feet by 8 feet. Therefore, the dimension of the side of a large piece of furniture like an armoire will rarely be larger than 24 inches, so that one piece of plywood can be used to create both sides. It is possible to get 4-feet-by-10-feet plywood, but most lumber yards will need to special order it. Plywood also comes in a 5-feet-by-5-feet size, but this size is for Baltic birch only, which is used for drawer box construction.

Fiberboard

Medium-Density Fiberboard

Medium-density fiberboard, or MDF, is an engineered product using fine softwood fibers, wax, and resin to form a sheet product. MDF is not to be confused with particleboard, which has larger particles as its core and is used for low-end furniture. Standard thicknesses of MDF for furniture construction are ¼ inch, ½ inch, ¾ inch, and 1 inch. The boards are available in 4-feet-by-8-feet sheets. This material is typically used for contemporary designs for which veneer is needed because it has a flat finished surface for gluing and is a stable material. It also can be shaped easily with routers and shapers, making it a good material for painted and curved moldings. However, MDF is associated with health risks because it uses a formaldehyde resin in the material fabrication process.

High-Density Fiberboard

High-density fiberboard (HDF), or Masonite, is an engineered product using wood fibers to produce a harder, denser material than MDF for creating flat sheet goods. HDF is used for drawer bottoms and back panels in furniture.

Wheatboard

This is a manmade material constructed of recycled wheat chaff that is produced without formaldehyde, creating an emission-free board. This is also an alternative "green material" to MDF. These boards are becoming more widely used and are typically 10% lighter than standard particle board materials and are available in the same thickness and dimensions.

Bender Board

Bender board is used to create curves or bends in a piece of furniture. There are two basic types of bender board. The first is a plywood type that is available in 4-feet-by-8-feet sheets and is ⅜-inch thick with a total of three plies. It is the direction of the plies that makes it bendable by having the grain direction of the two outside plies run perpendicular to the curve that is created. This is because the wood bends easier in the grain direction. The second type is an MDF product that is available in 4-feet-by-8-feet sheets and is ⅜-inch thick, but it has slots cut into one side. (See Figure 3.7.) Both types of material needs to be doubled up to create a final thickness of ¾ inch.

Figures 3.8a through f show how the doors of a piece are created using bender board. To begin, a two-part mold is created for the piece. The bender board is placed between the mold's parts with wood glue, and while the glue is still wet, the mold is clamped together until the glue dries. When the glue is dry the bender board is removed from the mold and retains its shape. Veneer is then used to create the exterior surface. This is done before the finishing starts. Another way to create a piece using bender board

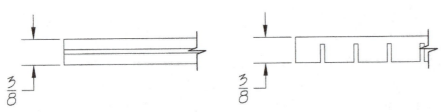

Fig. 3.7 Edge detail of plywood-style bender board and MDF-style bender board.

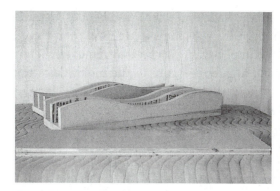

Fig. 3.8a Step 1. 2-part mold.

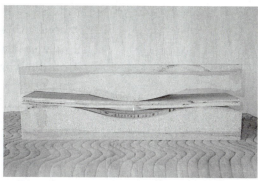

Fig. 3.8b Step 2. Bender board placed between the mold with wood glue still wet.

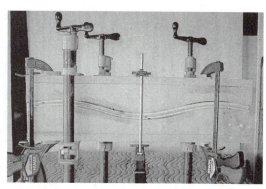

Fig. 3.8c Step 3. Mold is then clamped together until glue dries.

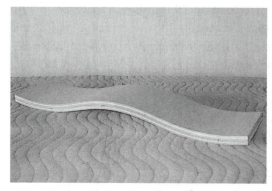

Fig. 3.8d Step 4. Bender board is now rigid when glue has dried. Shown out of mold.

Fig. 3.8e Example of finished piece; the process is repeated four times for these doors. Veneer is applied to all sides before the finishing starts.

is to use a mold and vacuum system. The bender board is placed into a mold with the glue still wet and then placed into a special vacuum bag. A compressor removes the air from the bag and applies pressure to the mold. Once the glue dries, the mold is removed from the bag, and the bender board retains the shape from the mold.

Laminate

Laminate is a surface material that is generally $\frac{1}{16}$-inch to $\frac{1}{8}$-inch thick and is available in a wide range of finishes and finish materials. Plastic laminate is typically used because of the extensive finish choices from solid color, faux wood grains, and species type to different textures and surface patterns. Plastic laminate is manufactured with a thin wood backing for support. This is the same material used for kitchen countertops. Metal laminate is available typically with or without wood backing. The metal laminate can be prefinished with choices ranging from textures to brushed marks. The laminate is mounted to a substrate material such as MDF or bender board for curved surfaces and is typically glued with contact cement. Laminate is used in residential homes and in commercial projects for countertops, desk panels, and hotel surface tops because of its durability and resistance to water spills.

Metal

Ferrous Metals

The term "ferrous" is derived from the Latin word *ferrum,* which means containing iron. All ferrous metals contain iron, whereas nonferrous metals do not. The typical ferrous metal used in furniture construction is steel. Steel is a refined product created from iron and is available in many different forms from a metal supplier. Typically, steel can be found as a sheet, angle, rod, bar, and tubing. Tubing will come either round, square, or rectangular with two different dimensions: ID (inside dimension) and OD (outside dimension).

Steel can be connected to itself in three different ways. First is by welding, in which the joint of two pieces of steel is brought to its melting temperature and another piece of steel rod or wire is melted into it, joining the two pieces. Second is by brazing, in which two pieces of steel are heated and brass is melted into the joint. There is less cleanup required with this joint, but it is not as strong as welding and should not be used for anything structural. The third way is by cold connection, which means that heat is not applied to the joint. The pieces can be bolted or riveted together. Riveting involves drilling through the metal pieces and placing a rod or rivet in the hole. By hammering the rivet on each side, it mushrooms out and connects the two pieces. (See Figure 3.9.)

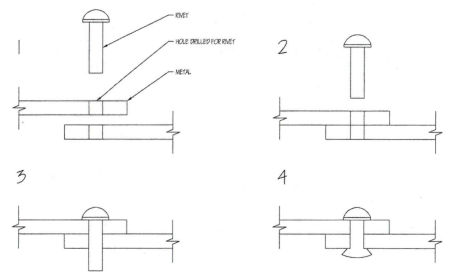

Fig. 3.9 How the rivet process works.

Nonferrous Metals

Typical nonferrous metals used in furniture are copper, brass, and bronze. These metals are soldered instead of welded. Soldering involves connecting metals by heating them to the solder's melting point. The solder flows into the joint, connecting the metals. The melting temperature depends on the type of solder. Tin solders melt around 400 degrees Fahrenheit, whereas silver solders melt around 1,400 degrees Fahrenheit.

Another way to connect these metals is to use a cold connection with bolts or rivets, as is done with ferrous metals.

A third process is to manipulate the metal through casting. Casting requires melting the metal into a liquid state and casting it into a mold. Figure 3.10 shows the casting process. The mold is a negative image of the final piece and is typically made from plaster or sand. This process starts with a wax part that is placed inside a steel cylinder. The wax item is connected to the bottom of the cylinder by another piece of wax called a gate. The gate allows the metal to travel to the item that will be cast. Then the cylinder is filled with plaster and heated in a kiln, which melts out the wax. The cylinder is then pulled from the kiln, and heated and liquefied metal is poured in. The final step is to clean the piece and cut off the gate. Casting is typically used in furniture to reproduce drawer pulls.

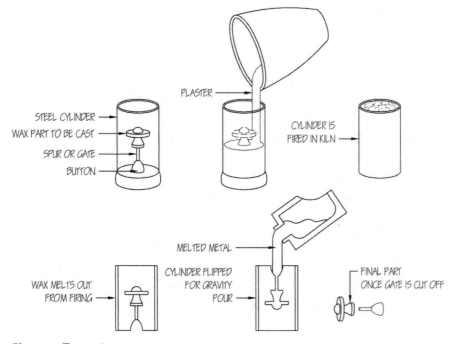

STEEL CYLINDER

WAX PART TO BE CAST

SPUR OR GATE

BUTTON

PLASTER

CYLINDER IS FIRED IN KILN

WAX MELTS OUT FROM FIRING

CYLINDER FLIPPED FOR GRAVITY POUR

MELTED METAL

FINAL PART ONCE GATE IS CUT OFF

Fig. 3.10 The casting process.

Chapter 3 Project and Quiz

Project

WOOD DIRECTORY

A wood directory is a visual directory of hardwoods and softwoods that contains characteristics and basic information about the wood so that you can distinguish one wood from another and know their common uses.

Directions: This assignment is a minimum of 21 pages (one page for each type of wood) and a cover page with "Wood Directory" and your name. On each page, include the following:

1. Name of the wood
2. Hardwood or softwood
3. Source of the wood (e.g., United States, Canada)
4. Appearance (e.g., color, texture)
5. Price per board foot
6. Common uses (e.g., furniture, cabinets, flooring)
7. Sample photo of the wood (color copy or Internet image)

The name of the wood should be font size 26; all other information should be font size 14. Of the 20 woods in your directory, show at least 15 hardwoods and 5 soft-woods. Include the following woods in your directory:

Hardwoods: alder, beech, cherry, hickory, mahogany, maple, oak, poplar, teak, walnut, and five others
Softwoods: cedar, Douglas fir, pine, and two others

AFRICAN PADAUK
Hardwood from West Africa

This wood has rich red-orange/purple-brown tones with red streaks in the grain. The grain pattern is straight to interlocking with a moderately coarse texture.

Price per board foot (bf): $8.99 as of 1/4/08

Common uses: interior joinery, furniture, turning, and flooring

Fig. 3.11 Example of page in a wood directory.

Quiz

Directions: Circle the best answer choice for each of the following questions.

1. Hardwood trees have
    A. leaves   B. needles

2. Which type of wood is good for taking paint?
    A. cherry   B. red oak   C. poplar

3. Which type of wood is good for outdoor furniture because of its natural oils?
    A. maple   B. teak   C. walnut

4. Match the section of the log to its description.
    A. pith   _____ transports nutrients
    B. heartwood   _____ outer protective layer
    C. sapwood   _____ center of log
    D. bark   _____ structural part of the trunk

5. What is the actual size of 4/4 lumber?
    A. ¾″ B. 1″   C. 1½″

6. What is a one board foot dimension based on?
    A. 12″ × 12″ × 12″ thick
    B. 12″ × 12″ × 1″ thick
    C. 12″ × 12″ × 2″ thick

7. What does MDF stand for?
    A. medium-density fiberboard
    B. maximum-density fiberboard
    C. milled-density fiberboard

8. What size is standard plywood available in?
   A. 36″ × 60″   B. 48″ × 72″   C. 48″ × 96″

9. What thickness is bender board typically available in?
   A. 1″   B. ¾″   C. ⅜″

10. Which of the following is a ferrous metal?
    A. brass   B. copper   C. steel

CHAPTER 4

Joinery

THIS CHAPTER FOCUSES on how wood furniture is joined together. It contains isometric and exploded drawings of the assembled joints and explains the strengths and uses of each joint.

Typically, joints are adhered with wood glue, which is a water-based glue. The joints are then compressed with clamps while the glue sets up. Because the glue is water-based it is naturally pulled into the fibers of the wood, which adds to the strength of the piece. Once the glue dries, the clamps are removed. Generally when a joint fails (breaks apart) it occurs on either side of the glued area. This is because contemporary glue technology provides a strong bond that allows the wood to hold up to stress.

Basic Types of Wood Joinery

This chapter illustrates the variety of wood joinery, which developed from the natural characteristics of wood. Each joint has strengths and weakness that make it suitable for a particular use. The joints are listed from simple construction to more complex, but the type used also depends on the application and design of the piece.

Butt Joint

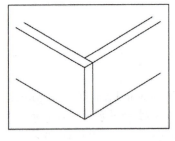
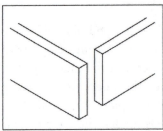

Fig. 4.1a An assembled and exploded butt joint.

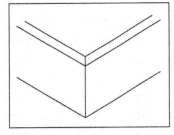
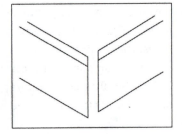

Fig. 4.1b An assembled and exploded mitered butt joint.

A butt joint is the simplest joint to use; it requires gluing one piece to another by butting them against each other and then clamping. This is not a strong joint, however, because the glue adheres to only one flat surface. A butt joint can be used in a square-edge joint for small boxes, and a mitered butt joint can be used for picture frames or in projects where you do not want the end grain to show. (See Figures 4.1a and 4.1b.) The butt joint can be reinforced with dowels (see dowel joint), biscuits (see biscuit joint), or screws. In applications where screws are used the joint is also glued and the screws are placed where they will not be seen. For example, the top of the piece is added to cover the screws that hold the base together.

Table 4.1
Basic Joint Applications

Joint | Recommended Application

Butt Joint   Small picture frames, small boxes

Loose-Tongued Joint   Large picture frames

Rabbet Joint   Drawer boxes (sides), cabinet construction

Dado Joint   Drawer boxes (bottom), shelves, cabinet construction

Edge-to-Edge Joint   Solid wood tabletops and panels

Tongue-and-Groove Joint   Solid wood tabletops and panels

Loose Tongue-and-Groove Joint   Solid wood tabletops and panels

Mortise-and-Tenon Joint   Leg-to-apron connections, cabinet construction

Through Mortise-and-Tenon Joint   Leg-to-apron connections, cabinet construction

Wedged Mortise-and-Tenon Joint   Decorative leg-to-apron connections

Loose-Wedged Mortise-and-Tenon Joint   Removable stretcher for tables

Dowel Joint   Solid wood tabletops and panels, cabinet construction

Biscuit Joint   Solid wood tabletops and panels, cabinet construction

Finger Joint   Drawer boxes (sides), cabinet construction

Dovetail Joint   Drawer boxes (sides), cabinet construction

Butterfly Joint   Solid wood tabletops and panels

Bridle Joint   Leg-to-apron connections, cabinet construction

Lap Joint   Stretcher between table legs

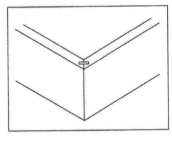

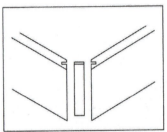

Fig. 4.2 A loose-tongued joint assembled and exploded.

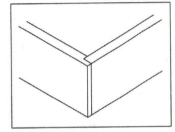

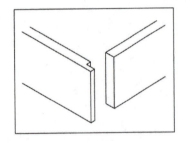

Fig. 4.3 Isometric view of a rabbet joint assembled and exploded.

Loose-Tongued Joint

For a loose-tongued joint, a piece of wood is added to the standard butt joint to create a stronger joint. Now, instead of the wood pieces butting against one another, material is removed for an extra piece to be glued between them. Many picture frames are produced this way. (See Figure 4.2.)

Rabbet Joint

A rabbet joint has material removed from the edge of one piece of wood so that the other piece can fit in square. It is used for creating drawer box corners and in cabinet construction. (See Figure 4.3.)

Dado Joint

A dado joint has material removed from one piece that is the same thickness as the material that will be jointed to it. This groove creates a tight bond between the two pieces. It is used for cabinet construction as well as for door and drawer elements. (See Figure 4.4.)

Edge-to-Edge Joint

This butt joint creates larger surface planes from smaller boards for tabletops and door panels. Because wood boards will expand and contract differently from one another, they are arranged so that the growth-ring direction for each board runs in the opposite direction of the one next to it. (See Figures 4.5a through d.)

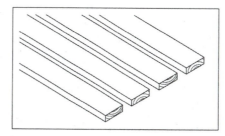

Fig. 4.5a Isometric view of an edge-to-edge joint exploded.

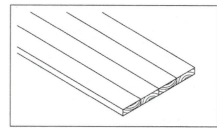

Fig. 4.5b Isometric view of an edge-to-edge joint assembled.

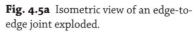

Fig. 4.5c Side view showing end grain detail exploded.

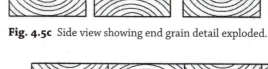

Fig. 4.5d Side view showing end grain detail assembled.

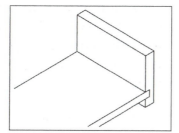

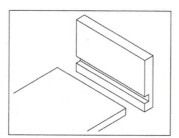

Fig. 4.4 Isometric view of a dado joint assembled and exploded.

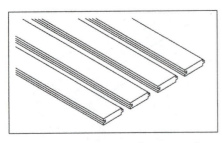

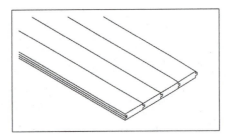

Fig. 4.6a Isometric view of tongue-and-groove joint exploded.

Fig. 4.6b Isometric view of tongue-and-groove joint assembled.

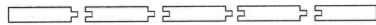

Fig. 4.6c Side view showing detail exploded.

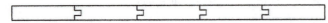

Fig. 4.6d Side view showing detail assembled.

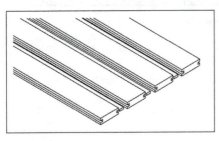

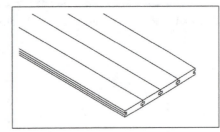

Fig. 4.7a Isometric view of loose tongue-and-groove joint exploded.

Fig. 4.7b Isometric view of loose tongue-and-groove joint assembled.

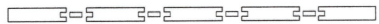

Fig. 4.7c Side view showing detail exploded.

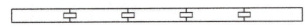

Fig. 4.7d Side view showing detail assembled.

Tongue-and-Groove Joint

A tongue-and-groove joint has a dado cut from one edge and a tongue or tab cut into the other. This creates a large glue surface with a tightly fitting edge. This style of joint is used in tabletop construction and wood flooring. (See Figures 4.6a through d.)

Loose Tongue-and-Groove Joint

This is similar to the tongue-and-groove joint except a dado is cut into each edge with a third piece of wood connecting the glue joint together. This style of joint, like the tongue-and-groove joint, is used in tabletop construction. In many cases, the end grain is visible so that the joint becomes part of the visual detail of the table. (See Figures 4.7a through d.)

Mortise-and-Tenon Joint

A mortise-and-tenon joint has a square notch (the mortise) cut out from one piece so that the other piece, which contains the removed material (the tenon), can fit into the mortise. The mortise is cut halfway through the material so that two tenons can connect on either side of the mortise. The end of the tenon is also mitered. This is a common joint for table and chair legs to connect to the rail. (See Figure 4.8.)

Through Mortise-and-Tenon Joint

This type of mortise-and-tenon joint has a square notch cut all the way through one piece so that the tenon can fit into the mortise through to the opposite side. This is a common joint for Arts and Crafts-style furniture. (See Figure 4.9.)

Wedged Mortise-and-Tenon Joint

This type of joint is similar to the through mortise-and-tenon joint, but a cut is made to the tenon so that a wedge can be added. This adds pressure to the glue joint, which makes it stronger. This joint is used commonly in Arts and Crafts–style furniture. (See Figure 4.10.)

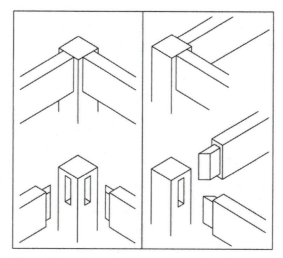

Fig. 4.8 Two different views of a mortise-and-tenon joint.

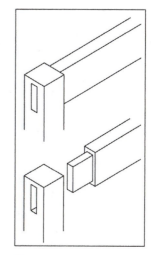

Fig. 4.9 Isometric view of a through mortise-and-tenon joint where the end grains form the tenon and becomes part of the decorative detail of the joint.

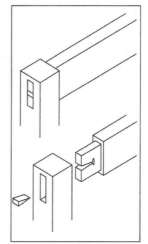

Fig. 4.10 Isometric view of a wedged mortise-and-tenon joint.

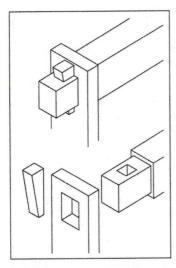

Fig. 4.11 Isometric view of a loose-wedge mortise-and-tenon joint.

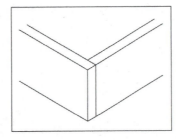

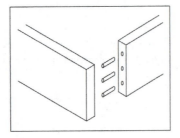

Fig. 4.12 Isometric views of a dowel joint exploded and assembled. When joint is glued, the dowels are concealed inside the joint.

Loose-Wedged Mortise-and-Tenon Joint

The loose-wedged mortise-and-tenon joint uses the same principle as a mortise-and-tenon joint, except that a wedge is added to pin the joint together through the tenon without glue. The tenon is longer than the mortise to allow room for the wedge. This type of joint is typically used in large pieces, such as a trestle table, that need to be disassembled to get through doorways. (See Figure 4.11.)

Dowel Joint

This type of joint has wood dowels fit into drilled holes where two pieces will be joined together. The dowels expand slightly in the holes because of the water-based wood glue. This joint is used by many furniture manufacturers because of its low cost for mass-market manufacturing. It is also found in Ready to Assemble (RTA) furniture, also known as Knock Down (KD) furniture. With this type of furniture, the end user assembles the finished components. (See Figure 4.12.)

Biscuit Joint

This joint is also widely used by manufacturers because it is faster to produce than the dowel joint. Basically, a biscuit-cutter hand tool is used to make a small groove in

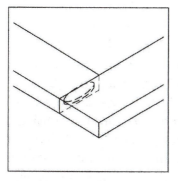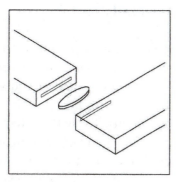

Fig. 4.13 Isometric views of a biscuit joint exploded and assembled.

both pieces of material, and then a biscuit (a small oval piece of material) is added into the groove with glue. The piece is clamped until the glue dries, allowing the biscuit to slightly expand in the groove, which creates a tight joint. The biscuit joint is found in case-and-frame construction. (See Figure 4.13.)

Finger Joint

A finger joint has equal amounts of material removed from both pieces of wood. This creates a finger detail at the end of the material, which is a combination of solids and voids that have been cut at a right angle to allow these pieces to slide together. This type of joint is also found in case-and-frame construction when the joint is designed to be part of the furniture's detail. (See Figures 4.14a and 4.14b.)

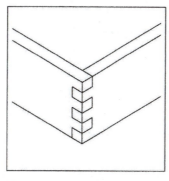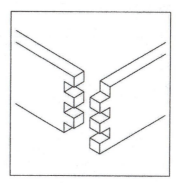

Fig. 4.14a Isometric views of a finger joint exploded and assembled.

Fig. 4.14b Side view of a finger joint.

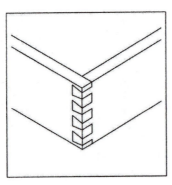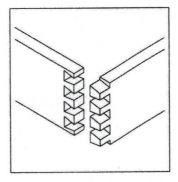

Fig. 4.15a Isometric views of a dovetail joint exploded and assembled.

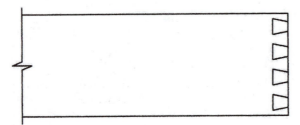

Fig. 4.15b Side view of a dovetail joint.

Dovetail Joint

A dovetail joint is similar to a finger joint, but the material is cut at an angle instead of straight. This creates a strong joint for drawer and cabinet construction. Dovetail joints used to be cut with a hand saw, which was time-consuming. Today they are produced with a router using a dovetail bit and jig. (See Figures 4.15a and 4.15b.) There are many types of dovetail joints. The two main types are the through dovetail and the half-blind dovetail. The through dovetail is constructed so that the joint can be seen on the two edges of the joint. The half-blind dovetail is constructed so that one edge is cut halfway through. This creates a joint that can be seen on one edge only.

Butterfly Joint

This type of joint is used to add strength when joining boards together. It is basically one piece of wood that looks like two connecting dovetails. It adds to the strength of boards that are glued edge to edge and is typically found in Arts and Crafts–style furniture. (See Figures 4.16a through d.)

Bridle Joint

This joint is similar to a mortise-and-tenon joint. The main difference is that the mortise is cut at the end of the material rather than being an enclosed square hole. The tenon piece is cut to fit into that mortise. There are two basic types of bridle joints, the corner bridle and the T bridle. These joints are used in chair and table construction. (See Figures 4.17a and 4.17b.)

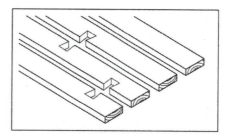

Fig. 4.16a Isometric view of a butterfly joint exploded.

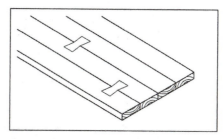

Fig. 4.16b Isometric view of a butterfly joint assembled.

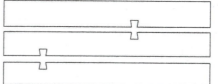

Fig. 4.16c Top view of a butterfly joint exploded.

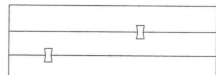

Fig. 4.16d Top view of a butterfly joint assembled.

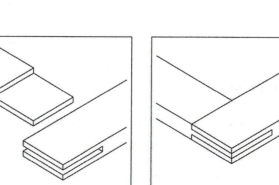

Fig. 4.17a Isometric views of a corner bridle joint exploded and assembled.

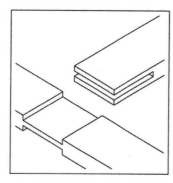
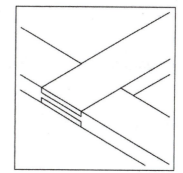

Fig. 4.17b Isometric views of a T bridle joint exploded and assembled.

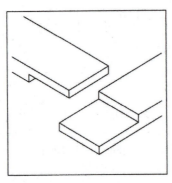
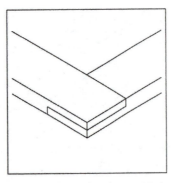

Fig. 4.18a Isometric views of corner lap joint exploded and assembled.

Lap Joint

This joint is similar to a rabbet joint. The difference is that 50 percent of the material is removed from each piece. This allows the pieces to overlap each other while maintaining the same overall thickness of the material. The lap joint is used in tables to connect the bottom portion of the legs with stringers or when creating latticework in wine racks. There are three basic types of lap joints: the corner lap, the T lap, and the cross lap, which are chosen by their application. (See Figures 4.18a through c.)

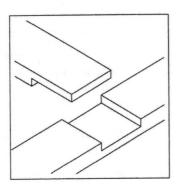
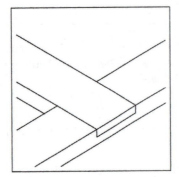

Fig. 4.18b Isometric views of T lap joint exploded and assembled.

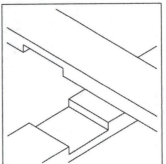

Fig. 4.18c Isometric views of cross lap joint exploded and assembled.

Chapter 4 Project and Quiz

Project

JOINT DIRECTORY

A joint directory is a visual directory of furniture joints that contains each joint's characteristics and basic information of where it is used so that students will be able to design structurally sound furniture.

Directions: This assignment is a minimum of 15 pages (one page for each joint plus a cover page with "Joint Directory" and your name). On each page, include the following:

1. Name of the joint
2. Common uses (e.g., face frame assembly)
3. Two drawings of the joint (e.g., isometric view exploded and assembled)

Include the following joints in your directory:

1. Butt joint
2. Mitered butt joint
3. Rabbet joint
4. Lap joint (cross lap and corner lap or T lap)
5. Edge-to-edge joint (butt joint, tongue-and-groove): show grain (side view only)
6. Dado joint (stopped joint)

7. Mortise-and-tenon joint (through and stopped joint)
8. Double mortise-and-tenon joint
9. Wedged mortise-and-tenon joint
10. Loose-wedged mortise-and-tenon joint
11. Bridle joint
12. Dovetail joint (through and half-blind joint)
13. Dowel joint
14. Biscuit joint

Quiz

Directions: Give the name for each of the following joints.

1.

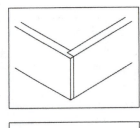

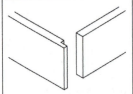

2.

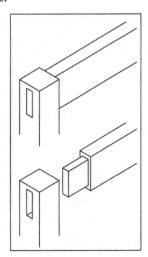

3.

4.

5.

6.

7.

8.

9.

10.

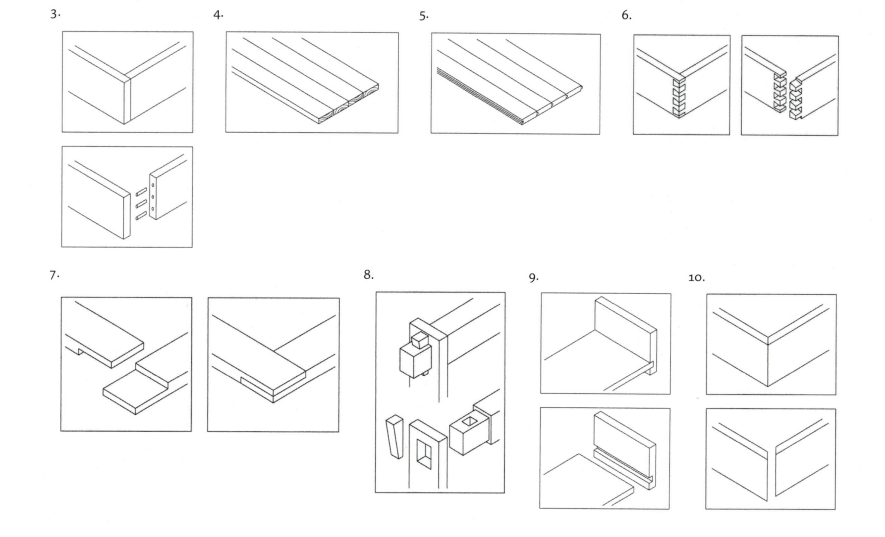

CHAPTER 5

Finishes

FOR MANY PIECES of custom furniture, the finishing process can take just as long as the building process. A common misconception is that finishing a piece of furniture simply adds color or shine to the piece. In reality, the purpose of finishing wood is to bring out the wood's beauty, revealing the color, depth, texture, and style of the grain. It also provides protection for the material from day-to-day use and the natural elements. This chapter shows the differences in stains, paints, oils, waxes, and clear coats, as well as how they are applied.

Prepping the Piece

For custom furniture, the fabricator constructs the complete piece using raw wood in a dry-fit stage, fitting all drawers, doors, shelves, and other components. This involves installing metal hardware, such as hinges and drawer slides, and checking the gap tolerances to make sure the piece is complete and up to the quality requirements of both the designer and fabricator. At this point, the piece is sanded with 80-grit sandpaper. The coarseness of sandpaper is based on a number system where the higher the number, the finer the sandpaper. (See Table 5.1.)

The piece is now ready to be disassembled in order to start the finishing process. Once the hinges, drawer slides, and the like have been removed, the piece is sanded with 150-grit sandpaper. This removes any scratches left from

Table 5.1
Sandpaper Grades

Coarseness	Grade	Uses
Very coarse	40 and 60 grit	Used in the building process
Coarse	80 and 100 grit	Used in the building process
Medium	120 and 150 grit	Used in prepping for finish
Fine	220 grit	Used in prepping for finish
Very fine	320 and 400 grit	Used in the finishing process

sanding with 80-grit sandpaper. The process is then repeated with 220-grit sandpaper, which will leave the surface feeling smooth. When the piece is completely sanded
with 220 grit, it is wiped down with a tack cloth to remove
any dust and is ready for the finishing process. (See Figures 5.1a through c.)

Fig. 5.1a Built-in hutch at raw
wood dry fit stage.

Fig. 5.1b Built-in hutch finished
and installed.

Fig. 5.1c Doors showing the difference between oak in raw wood and
golden oak oil-based stain.

Wood Finishes

There are many ways to finish wood, with choices ranging from the type of finish to the way it is applied to the surface. Six different finishing methods are discussed in this section: staining, glazing, painting, oiling, clear coating, and waxing.

Pigment Stains

Pigment stains are made from a finely ground pigment that creates a semitranslucent color that allows the wood's grain pattern to show through. However, pigment stains typically are used to change the color of the wood, which alters the original look of the material. These are widely available at home improvement centers and come in a ready-mixed color form. The color can also be changed or customized with a universal colorant tint (UTC). There are three basic types of stains available: water-based, alcohol-based, and oil-based; each type has its pros and cons.

WATER-BASED STAINS

Water-based stains use water as the material for delivering the pigment to the wood. The advantages of water-based stains are that they are easy to distribute any color evenly, they can be cleaned up with water, and they are earth-friendly. They also have a quick drying time of 15 minutes to 1 hour, depending on the humidity level. The main disadvantage to water-based stains is that the water raises the grain, just like putting a wooden spoon in the dishwasher. The material becomes slightly rough and will need to be sanded with 220- or 320-grit sandpaper. Resanding and the possibility of needing to apply a second coat can make using a water-based stain a very time-consuming process. Once the color is achieved, a sanding sealer can be applied that will seal the finish color before the top clear coat is applied. This step allows the top clear coat to dry on top of the surface rather than being absorbed into the material.

ALCOHOL-BASED STAINS

Alcohol-based stains use a methylated alcohol to transfer the pigment to the wood's surface. The alcohol dries very quickly, from 5 to 10 minutes, so the stain is typically sprayed onto the piece's surface. The alcohol will not raise the grain of the wood, but it is more difficult to use than water-based stains. A sanding sealer will be applied before a top clear-coat finish.

OIL-BASED STAINS

Oil-based stains use mineral spirits with an oil-based solvent, naptha, to transfer the pigment to the wood's surface. These types of stains dry quickly, from 10 to 30 minutes, and will not raise the grain. They are brushed on and wiped off to create an even finish. Typically, it is a one-coat process to create the basic color, but some brands of stain can be recoated to create a darker color with each additional layer.

Glaze

Glazes are pigmented wiping stains that are applied over the sanding sealer. Glazing is a process of changing the base finish by applying more layers of a glaze before the final clear coat. This process can be used to create more depth to the finish, for example, or to create an aged finish. The process can involve just one layer or many layers, depending on the desired look. Each layer is typically applied with a brush and then wiped off before it completely dries. The color change is accomplished because the glaze color is usually a contrasting tone from the base color.

Paint

Paint is an opaque coating that hides the wood's color or grain. The painting process is simple. Typically, for a new piece of furniture, the builder will use poplar because that type of wood absorbs paint evenly and has a low cost per board foot. Latex or any water-based paint can be brushed or sprayed on the surface and typically will not need a primer, depending on the color. When using darker shades of paint a primer may be needed to ensure an even tone. These water-based paints can be cleaned up with water and are better for the environment but will raise the wood's grain and need to be sanded between coats. For furniture, a flat paint finish is typically used because the final clear coat will create the final finish's desired luster.

For oil-based paints, a water-based primer should be applied first to seal the surface. Then the oil-based paint can be applied. Oil-based paints typically take from 6 to 24 hours to dry between coats, and they create a durable finish surface. The durability of oil-based paint makes it a good choice for pieces in high traffic areas that may get a lot of use, such as a dining table.

Oil

Tung oil is a wood-finishing product that is applied to raw wood to bring out the wood's natural color. It is applied with a rag by wiping on the oil and then buffing it dry. This process is repeated to create about five to six coats, with 6 to 12 hours of drying time between coats.

Salad-bowl oil finishes are applied to raw wood surfaces with which food will come in contact, such as butcher-block tops, bowls, and spoons. This type of oil is used because most oil finishes contain toxic materials and should never come in contact with anything used in the food preparation process. An alterative to buying a salad-bowl oil finish is to use any edible oil such as corn oil or olive oil. Both tung and salad-bowl oil will need to be reapplied once or twice a year to protect the wood.

Clear Coats

Clear coats are a final top coat that can add depth or change the overall luster of the piece and add protection. Clear coats come in three different types: lacquer, varnish, and polyurethane.

Lacquer is available in two basic types: nitrocellulose and catalyzed. Nitrocellulose lacquer is widely used in the furniture industry because it dries quickly, is completely clear, and will not change the color of the base finish. When using this finish, each layer of clear coat is partially redissolved by the next coat, creating a complete bond. Catalyzed lacquers are like automotive finishes in that they involve a two-part process. A resin and a hardener are mixed before applying the lacquer to the piece. Once mixed, a chemical reaction starts setting the lacquer. This type of lacquer creates a hard clear surface if the formula is mixed correctly, and it can be extremely toxic.

The other clear coat types are varnish, which is a dried oil resin and solvent mixture, and polyurethane, which is a product like varnish but made from a polymer and urethane structure, basically a liquid plastic. These finishes take much longer to dry, sometimes 6 to 24 hours, and can be applied with a brush or sprayed on. They are available in flat to gloss finishes and can be tinted with colorant to create a transparent color. They are also available in an exterior finish that can handle the elements; therefore, boat woodwork is typically finished in an exterior varnish that does not yellow as much as polyurethane does when exposed to the elements.

Wax

Wax finishes can be a good alterative to spray-on clear coats and are better for the environment, but they have limitations. The base for old wax products was beeswax mixed with other waxes and dissolved with a solvent, which was mixed by the furniture builder. Waxes today are available ready-mixed in liquid or paste form and are applied by wiping on the wax and then buffing the surface with a clean rag. Wax can be applied to raw wood, but generally it is used over an oil-based stained finish to seal the surface and add a soft luster. Over time, the wax must be reapplied, but the finish will continue to improve over the years. Waxes are also a good way to protect antiques. A note about antiques: The original finish on an antique is as important as the material itself. Therefore, protecting that finish protects the value of that piece.

Metal Finishes

Oxidation Process

Oxidation is a natural change in the metal due to exposure to oxygen in the air. Steel will rust, turning it a warm orange-brown tone. Copper will patinate, turning it a dark brown-bronze color and then a green-blue color. The oxidation process can be sped up with chemicals or by using natural ingredients. For example, copper will patinate a green-blue color by putting it in a sealed plastic bag with wood chips, ammonia, and salt. With any oxidation process, once the color is achieved, it needs to be sealed, which typically is done with a wax.

Heat Treated

Some nonferrous metals such as copper, brass, and bronze can be given a heat-treated finish. This is achieved by heating the metal slowly over the surface until the desired color is achieved. Once the metal has cooled to room temperature, it needs to be sealed with wax or a clear coat.

Abrasive Finishes

An abrasive finish can be applied to any type of metal by using an abrasive surface to alter the surface of the metal.

A brushed finish is created by sanding the metal in one direction so that the scratches from the sandpaper are all going in the same direction. An angle grinder has a spinning disk that can be used to create circular marks in the metal. Once the desired look is created the metal is sealed with a clear coat.

Powder Coat

The powder-coating process uses a colored powder that is given a positive electric charge. The metal part is given a negative electric charge. Then the powder is sprayed onto the metal, and the electrostatic charge allows the powder to stick to the metal part. Once the powder is attached to the metal, the part is baked in a kiln to fuse the powder to the metal surface. Then the piece is removed from the kiln, and the color is permanently attached. Powder-coated surfaces will not corrode from the elements, which makes them ideal for exterior applications.

Basic Furniture Hardware

Furniture hardware can range from decorative items, such as a knob, to mechanical items, such as hinges and drawer slides. This section illustrates many different types of hardware and the available options.

Door and Drawer Pulls

Drawer pulls can be broken down into three categories: knobs, handles, and bails. All of these perform the same function, which is to create a fixture in order to open or close a door or drawer. Deciding on one over the other is purely based on aesthetics. The knob is a single-style pull. (See Figure 5.2a.) It is typically held with a single screw from the back of the door or drawer. These parts are made of cast metal or turned wood, depending on the piece's style.

A handle has two connection points to the door or drawer and is connected in the same way as a knob with screws from the back of the door or drawer. Handles are typically metal but also are available in glass, plastic, and wood. (See Figure 5.2b.)

A bail is similar to a handle in the way it is mounted to the drawer. The difference is that bails have a hinge point on each side so that they swing. Bails are made from metal because of the strength of the material. (See Figure 5.2c.)

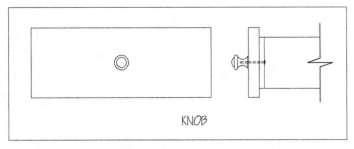

Fig. 5.2a A drawer from front and section view with knob.

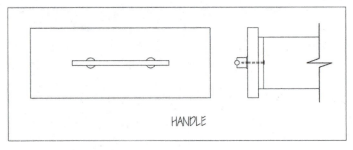

Fig. 5.2b A drawer from front and section view with handle.

An escutcheon is a back plate for a knob or a keyhole. This is a decorative item that mounts to the door or drawer behind the knob with a screw. Brad nails or small screws are used to secure the ends. (See Figure 5.2d.)

Door Catches

There are many different types of door catches. Which one to use for a project depends on how you want it to hold the door and how you want it to look. Most are based on a spring catch or a magnetic catch. (See Figures 5.3a through e.)

A ball catch has a pin that is attached to the door and a ball-bearing spring catch that is attached to the cabinet.

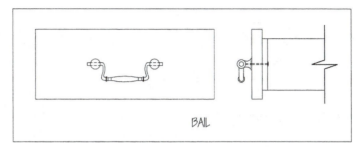

Fig. 5.2c A drawer from front and section view with bail.

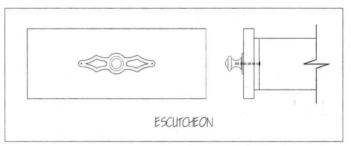

Fig. 5.2d A drawer from front and section view with escutcheon and knob.

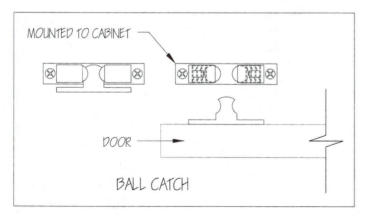

Fig. 5.3a A ball catch.

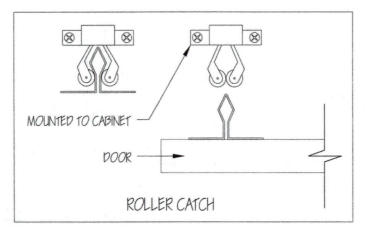

Fig. 5.3b A roller catch.

The casings for the springs and the pin are cast brass. The pin holds the door in place by applying pressure on each side of the catch.

A roller catch also has a pin attached to the door but has double rollers attached to the cabinet. When the door is closed, the double rollers hold the pin in place.

A magnetic catch has a magnet mounted to the cabinet or case and a steel pad mounted to the door. When the door is closed, the steel pad comes in contact with the magnet and holds the door closed.

A touch latch is used for doors that do not have a knob or handle. The user pushes the front of the door, and it

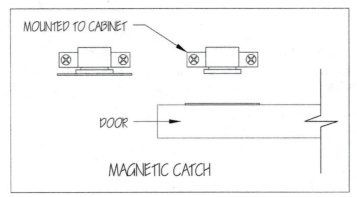

Fig. 5.3c A magnetic catch.

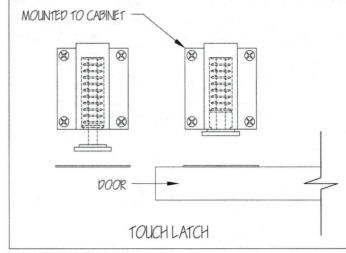

Fig. 5.3d A touch latch.

springs open. The latch is a magnet connected to a spring, and the door has a steel pad mounted to it. When the door is touched, the spring releases and breaks the magnetic bond with the door, thus opening the door.

A bullet catch has a cylinder with a ball bearing that is held with an internal spring that is drilled and mounted to the cabinet. The bottom edge of the door has a metal cup plate attached. This part attaches to the ball bearing when the door is closed, keeping it shut.

Glides

Glides are a part of a piece of furniture that is never seen. They mount to the bottom of the furniture to protect the piece when it is moved across a floor surface and also to protect the floor surface from being scratched. A typical glide is made from nylon and has a nail embedded into the plastic. This type of glide is simply nailed to the bottom surface of the furniture. (See Figure 5.4a.)

A leveling glide does the same thing as a nylon glide, but the plastic pad is mounted to a self-contained spring and set screw so that it can be adjusted to level the piece. (See Figure 5.4b.)

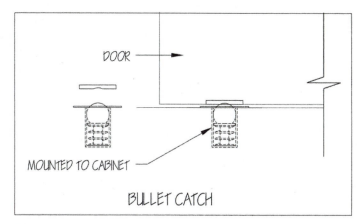

Fig. 5.3e A bullet catch.

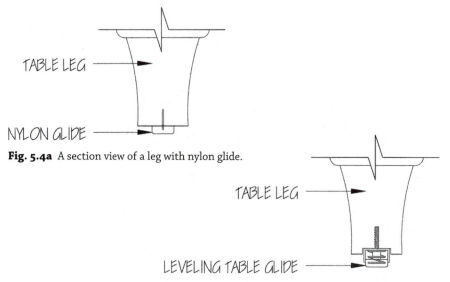

Fig. 5.4a A section view of a leg with nylon glide.

Fig. 5.4b A section view of a leg with leveling glide.

Shelf Supports

Shelf supports are used when the design calls for adjustable shelves. A shelf support peg is used on each corner of the shelf. Holes are drilled into the inside of the case deep enough to hold the pegs. Then the pegs are placed in the holes, and the shelf rests on the pegs.

Casters

Casters allow a piece of furniture such as a coffee table or butcher-block island to roll. Casters are available in different sizes based on the total weight they need to carry, as well as in different wheel diameters, fixed and swivel wheels, and lockable versions. The casters are mounted to the piece with screws through the flange, or they will have a rod that fits into a hole at the bottom of the piece. The total height of the caster includes the distance from the base of the wheel to the top of the flange. (See Figure 5.5.)

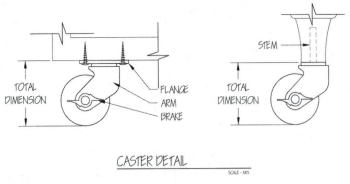

CASTER DETAIL

SCALE - NTS

Fig. 5.5 *Left,* a caster mounted to a flat base, such as a coffee table; *right,* a caster mounted to the base of a leg, such as an end table.

Chapter 5 Project and Quiz

Project

MARKER-RENDERING OF FINISHES

In this project, you will create a visual rendering of wood and metal finishes so that you will be able to create drawings for clients that communicate the finishes of materials.

Directions: Create renderings of three pieces of furniture based on color photographs of those pieces. Start by producing a line drawing with pencil, and then re-outline the image with a technical pen. Once the line drawing is finished, marker-render it to match the finish shown in the original photo, and use grey marker to change tones and add shadows. Figures 5.6a and 5.7a are photos of two different types of tables. Figures 5.6b and 5.7b are examples of marker-rendering finish materials.

Fig. 5.6a An end table.

Fig. 5.6b Black painted surface created with 20%, 40%, 60%, and 80% grey. Wood tone created with goldenrod to resemble photograph.

Fig. 5.7a Finished table.

Fig. 5.7b Marker rendering of finished table.

Quiz

Directions: Choose (or circle) the best answer for each of the following questions.

Match the grit numbers to the sandpaper.
1. Very coarse _____   A. 220
2. Coarse _____   B. 60
3. Medium _____   C. 320
4. Fine _____   D. 100
5. Very fine _____   E. 150

6. Which type of stain is the most earth-friendly?
    A. water-based   B. alcohol-based   C. oil-based

7. Which process does not need a clear coat?
    A. glazing   B. alcohol-based staining   C. waxing

8. Which type of wood is best for paint?
    A. teak   B. oak   C. poplar

9. Which type of lacquer involves a two-part process of resin and hardener?
    A. nitrocellulose   B. catalyzed

10. What does UTC stand for?
    A. unique color tint
    B. universal colorant tint
    C. universal color tone

Designing Furniture for Living Spaces

PART II

CHAPTER 6

Dining Room Furniture Design

THIS CHAPTER SHOWS how the different pieces of furniture included in a dining room are designed. The discussion starts with the dining table. You will see how a solid wood top and a veneered top are constructed, as well as different edge details. The chapter goes on to provide information about how round tops are created. Leg details, such as turned, tapered, and cabriole, are also discussed. In addition, you will see how to handle the complete construction of a typical dining table with leaves, a breadboard-style top, and a trestle table design, as well as how the base, legs, aprons, and top are joined together. This chapter also covers dining chair and armchair construction with different types of upholstery and concludes with storage pieces such as the buffet and china cabinet.

Dining Table

The dining table design should be based on the room itself. The size and shape of the table depends on the size and shape of the room with standard circulation clearances, as well as how the client expects the table to function. You need to know if the table is to seat four, six, or eight persons, and whether it needs to expand for special occasions.

When creating this piece of furniture, the most important dimension to consider is the work surface height. The top of the table should be 29 to 30 inches from the floor. The next important piece of information is how much tabletop space each person needs. The preferred dimension is 30 inches from elbow to elbow, but a minimum of 24 inches will also work. (See Figure 6.1.)

Table Parts

The basic parts to a dining table include the top, apron, legs, stretcher, and pedestal, depending on the style. (See Figure 6.2.)

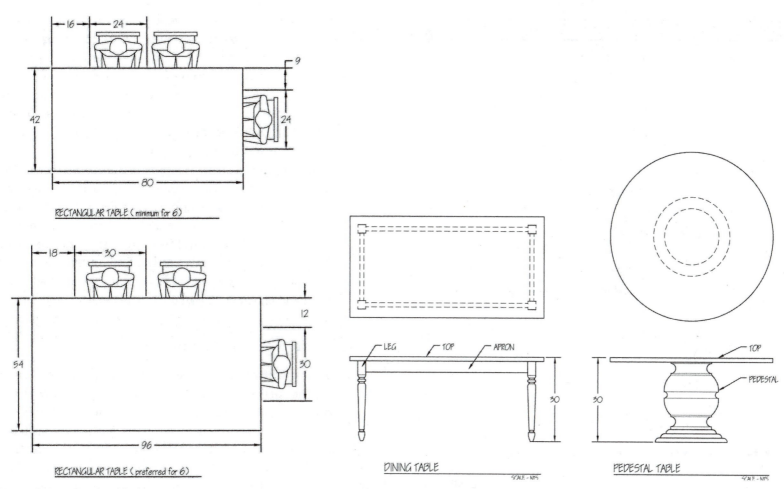

RECTANGULAR TABLE (minimum for 6)

RECTANGULAR TABLE (preferred for 6)

DINING TABLE
SCALE - NTS

PEDESTAL TABLE
SCALE - NTS

Fig. 6.1 Basic rectangle table dimensions.

Fig. 6.2 Basic table parts with dimensions.

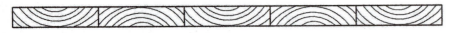

Fig. 6.3 Side view of wood grain direction.

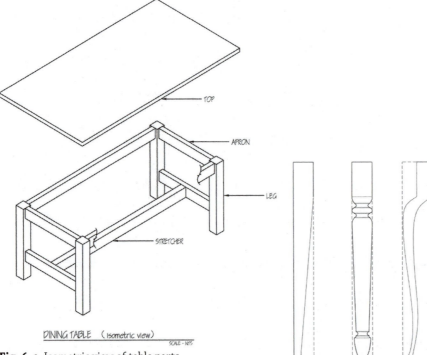

DINING TABLE (Isometric view)
SCALE - NTS

Fig. 6.4 Isometric view of table parts.

Fig. 6.5 Examples of a tapered leg, a turned leg, and a cabriole leg. The dashed area represents the overall material before the leg is cut out or turned on a lath.

The top can be solid wood, which consists of boards that are glued together to create the desired size. If the top is standard cut lumber, the end grain direction must be glued so that the grain of every other board is running in an opposite direction. This prevents warping. (See Figure 6.3.) The top can be made of veneer that has different grain patterns or can be made of some other type of material such as metal, stone, or glass.

The apron is a structural part of the table that connects the legs; together, the apron and legs form the base. Not all types of tables have aprons. (See Figure 6.4.) The leg is also a structural part of the table and can be created in a number of different ways, from the simple tapered leg to the turned leg to the cabriole leg. Each of these legs starts as a solid piece of wood, and material is subtracted to create the shape. (See Figure 6.5.)

SOLID WOOD TABLETOP

A solid wood top is constructed of many boards to create the total size of the top and is glued together edge to edge, tongue and groove, or with biscuits. The top is then sanded and connected to the base. For all dining tables, the top will not be glued to the base of the table; it will be attached with screws because the top needs to expand and contract independently from the rest of the table. A few different ways that the top can be connected is by using pocket screws, a metal angle, or a wood button.

- A pocket screw is screwed through an angled hole in the apron into the top.
- A metal angle is typically a piece of steel that is bent at a right angle with slotted holes in it. This piece is screwed through the slotted holes into the apron and top.
- A wood button is a block of wood that fits into a dado in the back of the apron and is screwed up into the top.

One final way to secure the top to the base is by using figure eights. These are similar to two steel washers that are connected, where one screw fits down into the apron while the other fits up into the bottom of the tabletop. (See Figures 6.6a through d.)

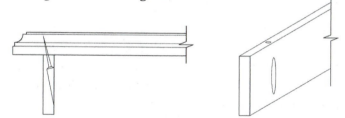

Fig. 6.6a Example of a pocket screw from section and isometric views.

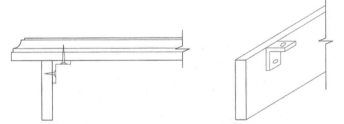

Fig. 6.6b Example of a metal angle from section and isometric views.

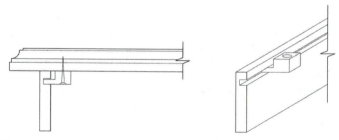

Fig. 6.6c Example of a wood button from section and isometric views.

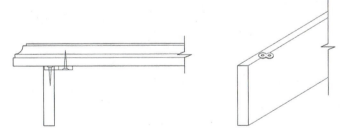

Fig. 6.6d Example of a figure eight from section and isometric views.

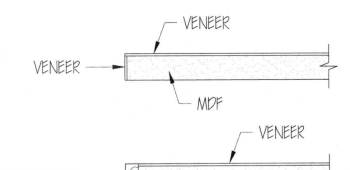

Fig. 6.7 Example of edge details.

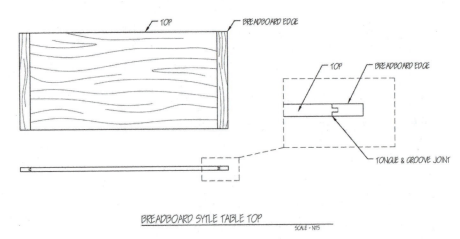

Fig. 6.8 Plan, elevation, and detail views of the edge.

VENEER TOP

Veneer tops will not expand or contract in the same way as solid wood tops because the veneer is glued to an MDF substrate material. Therefore, the top is screwed to the base without worry about how it may expand or contract. MDF is used because it is a stable material. The edge can be finished with veneer or with solid wood, which can take more abuse than veneer. (See Figure 6.7.)

BREADBOARD TOP

A breadboard top is made of solid wood. The long grain runs the length of the top and two end pieces are attached perpendicular to the rest of the tabletop. (See Figure 6.8.) This covers the end grain at each end of the tabletop and creates a detail to the top grain direction. These end pieces typically have a dado cut into them, creating a tongue-and-groove joint detail at the edge.

ROUND TOP

A solid wood round top is created by gluing wood boards together to make up a larger overall dimension and then cutting the top into a round form. (See Figure 6.9a.) This will provide a long grain on two areas and an end grain on the other two areas.

A plywood or veneer top with a solid wood edge is created by cutting an outside edge from solid wood, where the outside is made from eight equal pieces. (See Figure 6.9b.) This cuts down on waste and ensures that the long grain is the only part seen. These pieces are routed, so that the edge is a lap joint around the inside dimension. This lap joint is where the center plywood or veneer will fit.

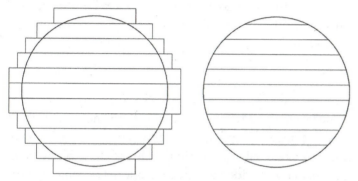

Fig. 6.9a Example of a solid round top, with board layout of a pedestal table on the left and final cut piece on the right.

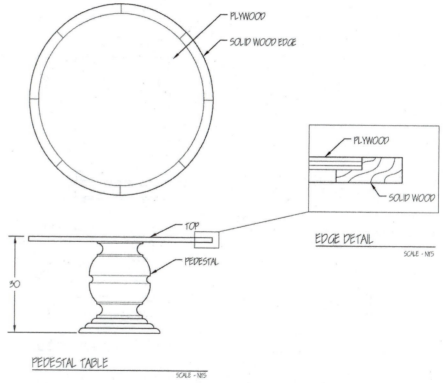

Fig. 6.9b Example of a plywood round top with solid wood edge.

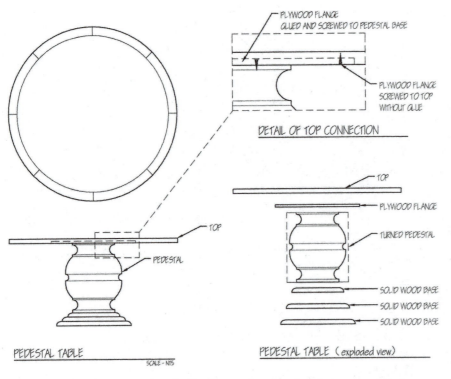

PLYWOOD FLANGE
GLUED AND SCREWED TO PEDESTAL BASE

PLYWOOD FLANGE
SCREWED TO TOP
WITHOUT GLUE

DETAIL OF TOP CONNECTION

TOP

PLYWOOD FLANGE

TURNED PEDESTAL

SOLID WOOD BASE
SOLID WOOD BASE
SOLID WOOD BASE

TOP

PEDESTAL

PEDESTAL TABLE
SCALE - NTS

PEDESTAL TABLE (exploded view)

Fig. 6.10 *Left*, a complete pedestal table; *lower right*, an exploded view; *top right*, the connection of top to base.

Table Types

Now that you understand the basic parts to a table and how the top is connected to the base, this next section shows how three other types of tables, the pedestal, trestle, and leaf, are constructed. The pedestal table has a single support unit holding the tabletop surface, the trestle table has two legs connected by a central stretcher, and the leaf table has the ability to expand to accommodate more people.

PEDESTAL TABLE

A pedestal table has a single structural mass at its base that supports the weight of the top. The base of the pedestal can be designed so that a single mass is the base, as long as it is wide enough to support the tabletop. The wider the top, the wider the base needs to be. The pedestal can also have legs for the base instead of a single flange. Smaller pedestal tables have three legs while larger tables will usually have four legs.

The pedestal is typically a turned piece with a flange at the top so that it can be attached to the tabletop. The flange is made of plywood and is screwed down into the pedestal, and then the flange top screws into the tabletop from underneath. If the pedestal does not have legs, the turned piece will be attached to a base made of solid wood. This piece can have a routed edge to it, depending on the style. The thickness is based on the thickness of the wood used and can be made up of stacked pieces to create a larger base. These pieces are screwed to each other and screwed to the base. (See Figure 6.10.)

TRESTLE TABLE

A trestle table has two structural posts that support the top. These supports will be connected with a stringer, also known as a stretcher. (See Figure 6.11a.) The stretcher is typically connected with a loose-wedge mortise and tenon. This allows the table to be broken down for shipping purposes as well as delivery into the home. (See Figure 6.11b.) With the stretcher attached, the table may not fit through doorways, so it needs to be able to be removed easily.

The posts have an upper base and a lower base made of solid wood. These pieces can be made from different widths and thicknesses to add detail and characteristics to the post structure. These pieces also spread out the weight, which makes the piece more stable. (See Figure 6.11c.)

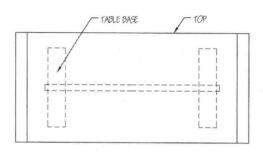

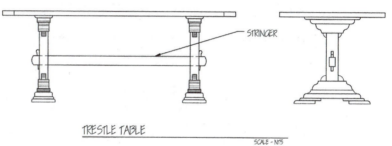

Fig. 6.11a A typical trestle table design.

Fig. 6.11b Detail of how a stringer is attached to a post with a loose wedge mortise and tenon.

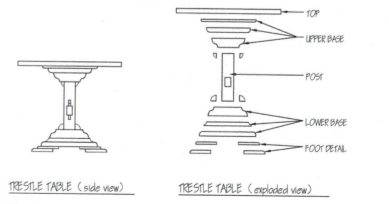

Fig. 6.11c *Left*, side view; *right*, an exploded view showing the solid wood parts.

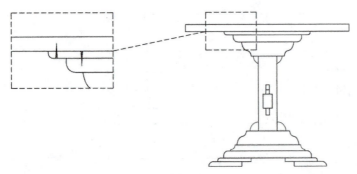

Fig. 6.11d Detail showing how top is attached with screws to base.

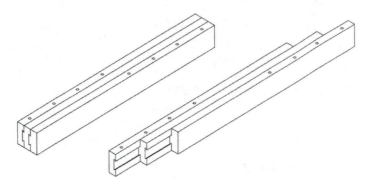

Fig. 6.12a A typical extension slide.

They also create the connection point from the base to the top. (See Figure 6.11d.)

LEAF TABLE

There are many different styles of leaf tables; however, they all have the same purpose, which is to increase the size of the table when needed. A traditional leaf-style table can be expanded in the middle by unlocking from the underside and pulling on each end of the table. (See Figure 6.12a.) The underside of the table is connected to two expandable extensions, typically made from wood with an interlocking dovetail. Individual leaves fit into the space provided by the extensions. A typical leaf is 12 inches wide, and depending on the table design, two, three, or four leaves can be added to increase the size up to 48 inches longer with all four leaves installed. (See Figures 6.12b and 6.12c.) Depending on the design of the table, the leaves may be able to be stored under the tabletop when not in use. There should be enough space between the aprons and between the extension slides of the table so that the leaves can be turned perpendicular to the top. They need to rest on a support bracket between the extension slides. This type of design typically will have leaves without aprons attached to them so that only the thickness of the leaves needs to be taken into consideration for spacing.

Another type of leaf table is a breadboard-style table. This is different than a standard breadboard table because the ends of this type of table are designed to slide out to

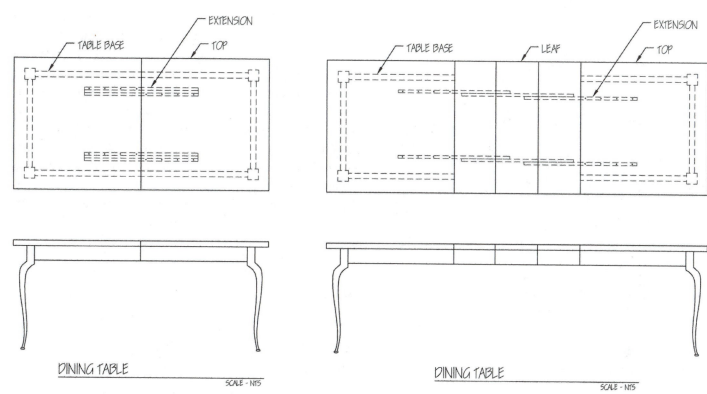

Fig. 6.12b Plan and elevation views of a dining table with closed extension slide.

Fig. 6.12c Plan and elevation views of a dining table with open extension slide.

121

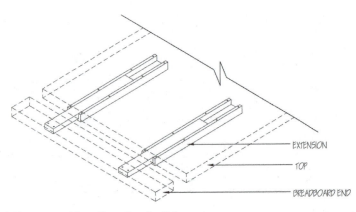

Fig. 6.13a A breadboard-style slide.

hold the leaf. This style is used when the base of the table is connected by a stretcher, so the base will not spread apart. This style uses breadboard ends, which are connected to two pieces of wood that slide into a box frame under the table. (See Figure 6.13a.) The breadboard ends slide out, and the leaves fit into each end. There are two drawbacks to breadboard tables. The first is that the table can only take two 12-inch-wide leaves, one for each side, thus only expanding the total table size by 24 inches. The second is that the base of the table does not move, so when the table is expanded the legs may be in the way, depending on the size of the table. (See Figures 6.13b and 6.13c.)

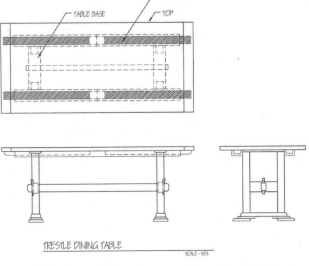

Fig. 6.13b Plan and elevation views of a breadboard dining table closed.

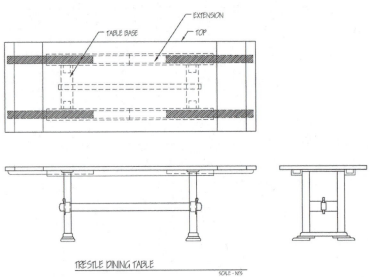

Fig. 6.13c Plan and elevation views of a breadboard dining table open.

Dining Chair

The ergonomics of dining chairs are based on human anthropometric measurements and proportions and the relationship between the user and the table. Dining chairs are one of the most difficult items to design because they must be comfortable; the designer must understand human ergonomics to be successful. Along with having the correct human dimensions, the designer must understand the proper angles and degrees. Incorrect angles can make the chair uncomfortable for long periods of sitting. This section also discusses how the quality of a chair's upholstery can explain how two identical chairs can be drastically different in price. Table 6.1 shows some basic dimensions and angles for a dining chair. (See also Figure 6.14.)

A chair must be structurally solid to support the weight of a person but still be light enough to be moved around the room. The wood frame of a typical dining room chair

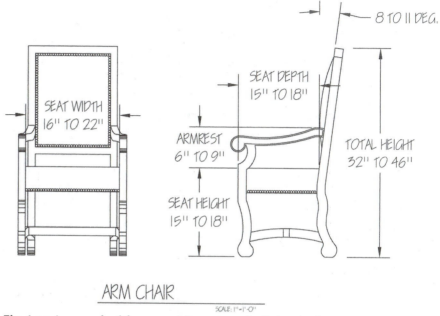

Fig. 6.14 An example of the range of dimensions of a dining armchair.

Table 6.1

Dining Chair Dimensions

Measurements	Purpose
15″ to 18″	Seat height from the floor
15″ to 18″	Seat depth
32″ to 46″	Overall chair height
16″ to 22″	Seat width (extra-wide chairs can be up to 26″)
6″ to 9″	Armrest height above the seat
8° to 11°	Angle for the back of the chair

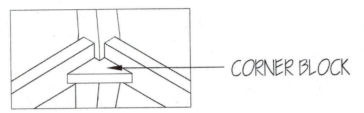

Fig. 6.15 Example of a corner detail of a chair.

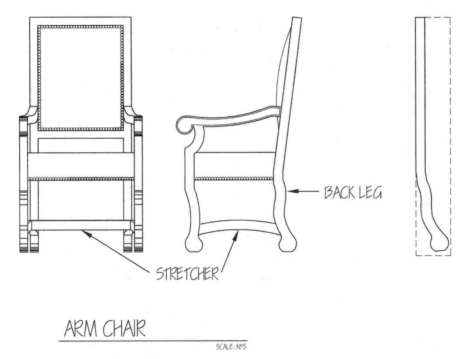

Fig. 6.16 A chair with stringers, and the side of the chair showing the back leg profile. The dashed line to the right shows the overall material that was used to create the back leg.

is constructed like a four-legged table base. The seat rails have a mortise-and-tenon joint at each end to connect them to the legs and have corner blocks to add strength. (See Figure 6.15.)

The back legs continue up to become the angle of the back of the chair. Each back leg should be cut from one piece of wood. (See Figure 6.16.) This gives the chair strength when weight is applied to the back of the chair. When dining chairs are designed for a hospitality environment, a stretcher can be added to the design. This adds strength to the overall design, which is important because these chairs may take more abuse than a typical dining chair. The chair in Figure 6.16 is a Louis XIV–style armchair that shows two types of stretchers. The first connects the front and back legs, adding strength from the front to the back. The second connects the right to the left, adding strength from side to side.

Most dining chairs have a larger dimension in the front of the seat than the back so that the seat is not a perfect square but tapers toward the back. Therefore, if the front of the seat is 23 inches wide, the back may taper down approximately 4 inches so the back dimension is 19 inches wide. (See Figure 6.17.)

Upholstery

When it comes to seat upholstery, there are many different options including grades, colors, and textures. The cost

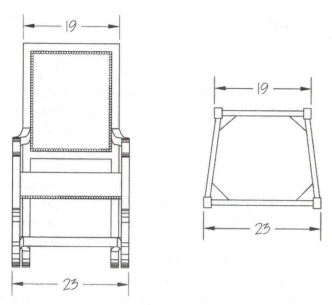

Fig. 6.17 Example of a chair from front elevation and a plan view of a chair frame.

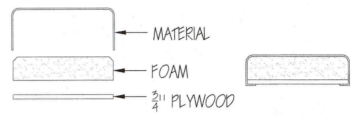

Fig. 6.18a An exploded section view and a section view of a drop-in seat.

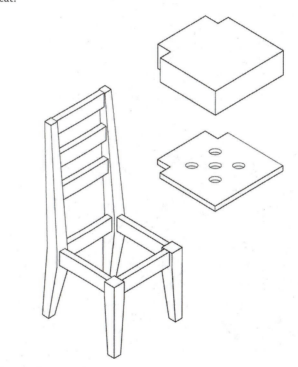

of the chair depends on the type of upholstery and cushion used. The first type is a drop-in seat, which is the least expensive style of seat. The seat is a completely upholstered piece that is attached to the chair with screws, typically through the corner blocks. It can be simply a piece of ¾-inch plywood with a foam cover, which is then covered with batting and the finish material. If the finish material is leather or vinyl, holes are drilled into the plywood so that the cushion can breathe when weight is applied. (See Figures 6.18a and 6.18b.)

Fig. 6.18b Example of a chair frame with plywood and foam in isometric view.

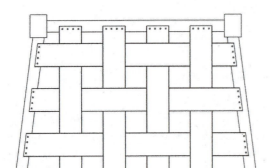

Fig. 6.19 Example of chair frame with webbing from plan view.

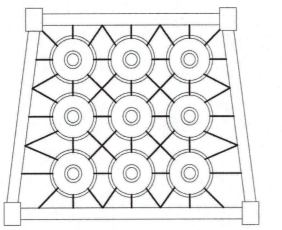

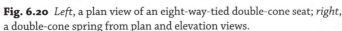

Fig. 6.20 *Left*, a plan view of an eight-way-tied double-cone seat; *right*, a double-cone spring from plan and elevation views.

One type of upgraded cushion has webbing attached to the top of the chair frame seat. (See Figure 6.19.) Then foam or another type of padding such as batting is added over the webbing. The finish material covers the padding and is wrapped around and attached to the underside of the chair frame. This makes the cushion nonremovable; therefore, the chair needs to have the final finish applied to the wood frame surface before upholstery begins.

Another upgraded cushion is a spring seat. (See Figure 6.20.) This type of cushion also has webbing attached to the bottom of the chair frame. Then double-cone springs are added on top with lashing, which means the springs are lashed or tied together and tied to the frame. This allows the springs to work as one complete system instead of as individual springs. This is where the term *eight-way tied springs* comes from, because each spring is tied from eight different directions. Padding is added over the springs, and then the finish material is attached to the frame.

For all of these cushion types, a bottom lining is added to the underside of the chair frame. This is a dust collector for the padding inside the chair frame; because of this bottom liner, all types of chairs look the same when you flip them over. It is the feel of the cushion that will tell what type of cushion it is.

Chair Back Construction: Zigzag Spring or Sinuous Wire Spring

The zigzag or sinuous wire spring is generally used for the back of a cushioned chair. The gauge or thickness of the wire used is determined by the intended load of the chair type and the overall height of the seat back. This is because of the distance that the wire has to travel from edge to edge of the chair frame. A longer distance may need a larger-gauge wire. The wire zigzags back and forth, creating a spring effect. (See Figure 6.21.) The spring is screwed to the frame of the chair, and lashing connects the springs together so that the springs work as one complete system. The springs are then covered by padding and then the finish material.

Buffet

The buffet is used as a storage and serving area for the dining room and typically matches the design elements of the dining table. Most designs will have drawers for storage of flatware and linens as well as lower doors for storage of larger items such as dishes and platters. Door construction typically includes three parts: stiles, rails, and a panel. (See Figures 6.22a and 6.22b.) The stiles are the two outside vertical pieces, and the rails fit horizontally

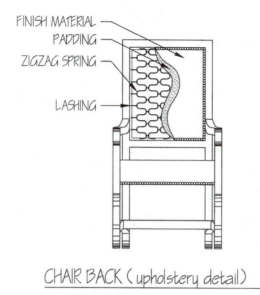

FINISH MATERIAL
PADDING
ZIGZAG SPRING
LASHING

CHAIR BACK (upholstery detail)

Fig. 6.21 Detail of an upholstered dining chair back with zigzag or sinuous wire spring. The lashing is to connect the springs, so that they will work as one complete system. The springs are covered by padding then the finish material.

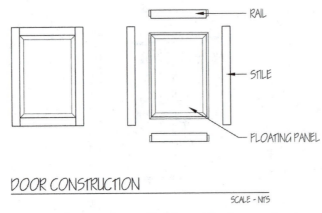

DOOR CONSTRUCTION

SCALE - NTS

Fig. 6.22a *Left,* a typical assembled door; *right,* the same door in exploded view.

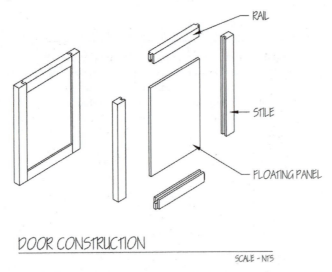

DOOR CONSTRUCTION

SCALE - NTS

Fig. 6.22b Typical door construction in both assembled and exploded isometric views.

between the stiles. The inside edge of these parts has a dado routed into the wood to hold the panel in place. The stiles and rails are glued together with the panel floating between them. The panel is not glued so that it can expand and contract. (See Figures 6.22c and 6.22d.)

The four basic stile and rail profiles are chamfer, bead, ogee, and radius. (See Figure 6.22e.) These profiles, along with the dado, are cut with a router or shaper where the bit on the cutting blade creates the desired profile. The images in Figure 6.22f show a standard square stile, which means that the edge of the stile is not shaped and a dado has been cut to hold the center panel. This square profile is used in Arts and Crafts and contemporary furniture.

The three additional images in Figure 6.22f show a typical flat panel door, a raised panel door, and a glass panel door. The flat panel door uses ¼-inch plywood for the panel, which fits into the dado. The raised panel door is made from ¾-inch solid wood that is glued together to create the desired size. The edge is routed to create a ¼-inch edge that will fit into the dado. There is also a ¹⁄₁₆-inch gap on the inside of the dado. (See Figure 6.22g.) This allows the panel to expand and contract with changing temperatures. The last section in Figure 6.22f shows a glass panel door that has a removable wood back edge so that the door can be finished before the glass is installed. This also allows the glass to be replaced if it breaks. The back edge of the wood is held in place with brad nails or small screws. These same types of connections are also used for any nonwood materials such as a metal sheet or screen.

Fig. 6.22c a typical door construction assembled (*left*) and exploded (*right*).

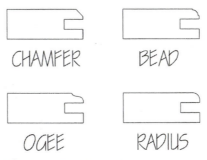

CHAMFER   BEAD

OGEE   RADIUS

Fig. 6.22e Four basic edge profiles for stiles and rails.

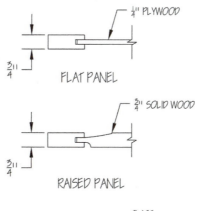

¼" PLYWOOD

¾"

FLAT PANEL

¾" SOLID WOOD

¾"

RAISED PANEL

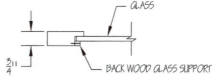

GLASS

¾"

BACK WOOD GLASS SUPPORT

GLASS PANEL

Fig. 6.22f Examples of a flat panel, raised panel, and glass panel door section.

Fig. 6.22d Fetail of a stile with raised panel and rail.

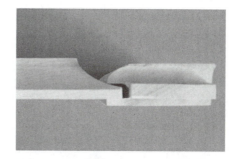

Fig. 6.22g Profile of a raised panel and end of rail before stile and rail are glued together.

Door and Cabinet Hardware

A buffet door can use a number of different hardware items, including hinges, knobs, and latching. (Knobs and latching are covered in Chapter 5.) The hinge can be part of the decorative details or can be hidden. A standard barrel-and-pin hinge is a simple way to hang the door and comes in many different sizes and finishes. They are also available in mortise and nonmortise styles. (See Figure 6.23.) A mortise-style hinge has material removed along the edge of the door where the hinge is placed. The non-mortise-style hinge does not need a mortise to be cut into the edge of the door; it fits into the gap between the door and the case.

If the hinge is not part of the details of the overall look of the piece, then a concealed hinge is the way to go. Concealed hinges fit into the back of the door and the inside of the case so that the hinges are not seen from the outside of the piece, and they can be adjusted if needed. These hinges are available in three basic styles: inset, overlay, and half-overlay. Which style to choose depends on how the door fits the piece of furniture. (See Figures 6.24a through c.) The inset hinged door fits inside the frame of the piece of furniture. The overlay hinged door fits in front and covers the complete face of the piece of furniture. The half-overlay hinged door is used when there are multiple doors that fit in front of the face. The half-overlay would be used on the inside doors, and the outside doors would have overlay hinges.

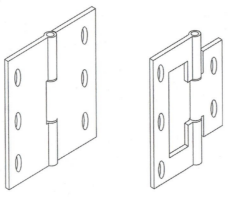

Fig. 6.23 Examples of a barrel hinge: *left*, a typical barrel hinge; *right*, a nonmortise-style hinge.

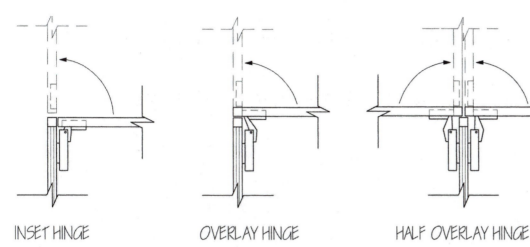

INSET HINGE   OVERLAY HINGE   HALF OVERLAY HINGE

Fig. 6.24a Example of an inset concealed hinge.

Fig. 6.24b Example of an overlay concealed hinge.

Fig. 6.24c Example of a half-overlay concealed hinge.

Custom Design and Modular Design

The interior designer can create any type, style, or dimension of buffet when ordering through a custom furniture builder. This is not typically possible with production furniture lines because most companies use modular pieces to create different lines. This means two different styles of furniture may use the same cut parts in each of these lines. Therefore, the tooling and cut list may be the same for 50 percent of the piece, which makes it impossible to change the dimensions or add details to these pieces. This is one way for a large manufacturer to keep costs down. The examples here show how modular design is possible

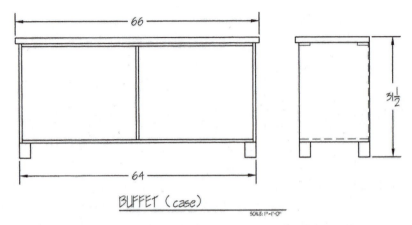

Fig. 6.25 Example of a ¾" plywood subframe construction.

using a subframe. Depending on the design, material is added to a subframe to create the overall styling. (See Figure 6.25.) This subframe is ¾-inch plywood that is skinned with solid wood. Each example shows how the subframe is changed. (See Figures 6.26a through g.)

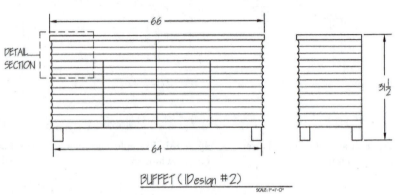

Fig. 6.26b A coved wood detail creating hidden drawers and doors.

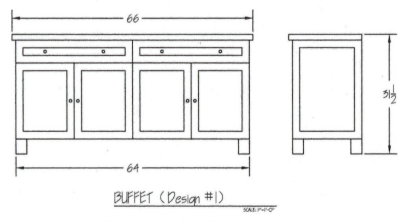

Fig. 6.26a A basic door and drawer with flat panel doors.

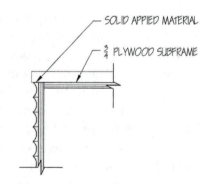

Fig. 6.26c Detail section of applied cove material.

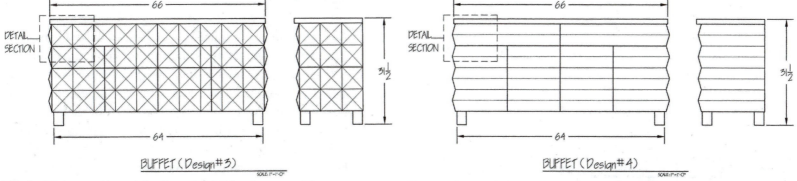

Fig. 6.26d A pyramid wood detail creating hidden drawers and doors.

Fig. 6.26f An angled wood detail creating hidden drawers and doors.

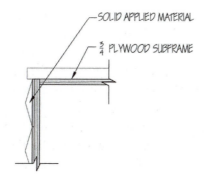

Fig. 6.26e Detail section of applied pyramid material.

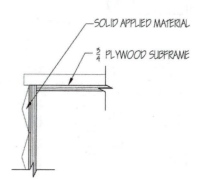

Fig. 6.26g Detail section of applied angle material.

133

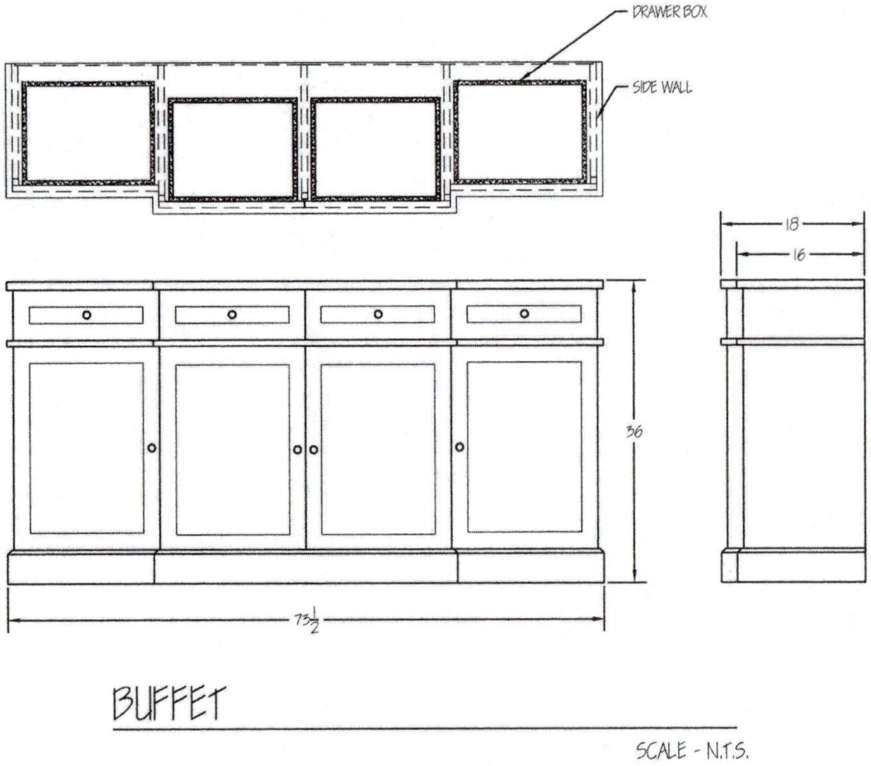

DRAWER BOX

SIDE WALL

18
16

36

73½

BUFFET

SCALE - N.T.S.

Fig. 6.27a A buffet.

China Cabinet

A china cabinet is similar to a buffet in that they are both used for storage in the dining room. The main difference is that a china cabinet is also used for display. It will typically be made up of two pieces for shipping and moving purposes. The lower piece is constructed like a buffet and the upper piece is a hutch that is mounted to the lower piece. (See Figures 6.27a and 6.27b.) These two pieces can be connected in many different ways. One way is to drill screws up into the hutch unit from under the top of the lower piece. However, this creates holes in the top that can be seen if the lower piece is not used with the upper piece. One way to avoid this is to design the cabinet with two pieces of wood that connect the upper and lower halves from the back. These pieces should be at least 36 inches long to give enough surface to connect to.

China cabinets have different types of molding, such as base and crown molding. The molding detail of any piece of furniture can be built up by layering different pieces of wood. The material will typically be ¾ inch thick; the molding detail for the china cabinet in Figure 6.27c uses three pieces, making it a total of 2¼ inches thick. Crown molding can be applied to the outside top structure of the piece. The molding material is cut with a molding machine to create its profile. The piece of molding is then cut to fit the piece of furniture and glued and nailed into place. In some cases, a reinforcing block can be added to the back of the crown molding. The molding will be mounted

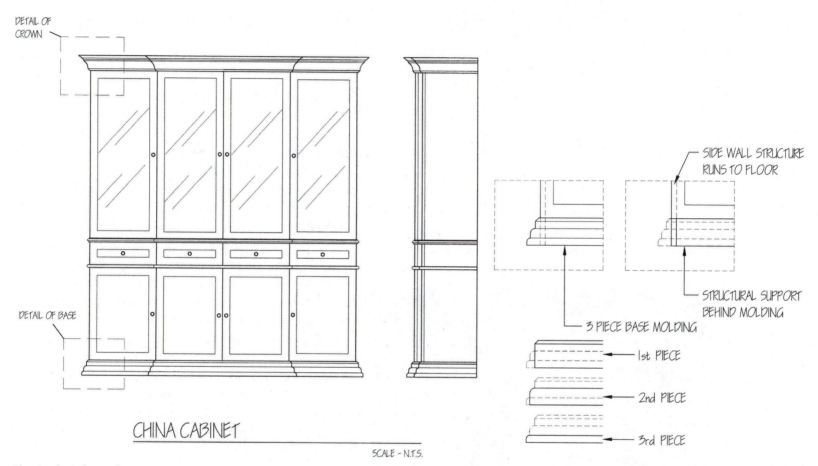

DETAIL OF CROWN

DETAIL OF BASE

CHINA CABINET

SCALE - N.T.S.

SIDE WALL STRUCTURE RUNS TO FLOOR

STRUCTURAL SUPPORT BEHIND MOLDING

3 PIECE BASE MOLDING

1st PIECE

2nd PIECE

3rd PIECE

Fig. 6.27b A china cabinet.

Fig. 6.27c *Top left*, a complete three-piece base molding; *top right*, the side wall comes to the floor with front support; *bottom*, each piece of ¾″ thick molding.

135

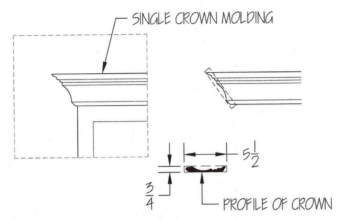

Fig. 6.28a Detail of crown molding, showing a single piece that has been cut with a shaper to create the profile. Original piece started as ¾″ × 5½″.

Fig. 6.28b The cabinet before crown molding.

Fig. 6.28c The cabinet with crown molding.

at a 45-degree angle to create volume. (See Figures 6.28a through c.)

The upper piece of the cabinet typically has glass doors for displaying items such as platters, dishes, and crystal. The china cabinet also may have a lighting system inside the top of the piece. Lighting companies create fixtures specifically for china cabinets. These are known as *puck lights* because they are basically the same shape and size as a hockey puck. The light is mounted inside the china cabinet, using either surface or recessed mounting, it is typically centered, and the wiring is mounted to the outside back of the piece. (See Figure 6.29.) Because the cabinet will most likely have multiple shelves, the shelves can be made from sheets of glass at least ¼ inch thick. The wider the cabinet, the thicker the glass needs to be, or there can be a wood frame with a glass insert. Glass allows the light to completely fill the cabinet. A basic rule for insetting glass or other materials in a wood frame such as a shelf is that the material should have a ¹⁄₁₆-inch gap on all sides. This will ensure a good fit. (See Figure 6.30.) The china cabinet shelves can also be designed with a groove along the back edge, approximately ¼ inch wide and ¼ inch deep. This edge will be able to hold plates and dishes vertically for display.

PLAN VIEW

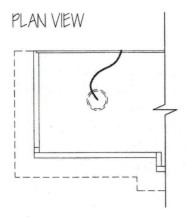

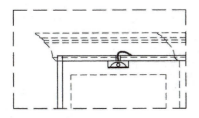

DETAIL SECTION
OF LIGHTING

Fig. 6.29 *Top*, placement of a puck light, centered in the door and front to back; *bottom*, a section view of a light and cord through the top of the cabinet.

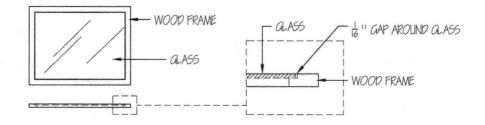

WOOD FRAME GLASS SHELF

SCALE - NTS

Fig. 6.30 Detail of a wood-frame-style glass shelf design. A basic rule for inset glass or other materials into a wood frame such as a shelf or top is that the material should have a $\frac{1}{16}''$ gap on all sides. This will ensure a good fit.

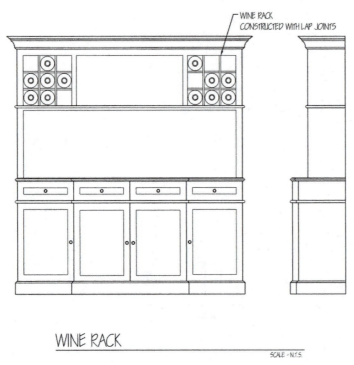

WINE RACK

Fig. 6.31a Example of a wine rack in a china cabinet.

Wine Rack

Another detail that can be added to a china cabinet is a wine rack. The main purpose of a wine rack is to create a display of wine that is easily accessible. This allows the wine to be kept at room temperature, which is ideal for red wines. The design should also display the bottle on its side so that the cork does not dry out, which allows the bottle to remain sealed. (See Figures 6.31a and 6.31b.)

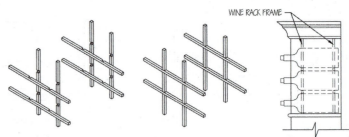

Fig. 6.31b Detail of a rack system. The first two images are isometric views showing the lap joint. The third image shows a side view of a rack with bottles.

Pie Safe or Food Cupboard

A pie safe is built in the same way as a buffet or cabinet. It typically has drawers at the top or base of the cabinet with two doors opening to a large interior space that has a couple of shelves. The distinctive feature of a pie safe is the tin punch panel doors. These doors are divided by center rails and contain metal panels that are placed into a rabbet from the back of the door. These metal panels have a punched-hole pattern to them, often of an American-style image such as an eagle or a star. The panels are tin (silver in color) or copper (orange in color), and the punched holes ventilate the cabinet. (See Figure 6.32.)

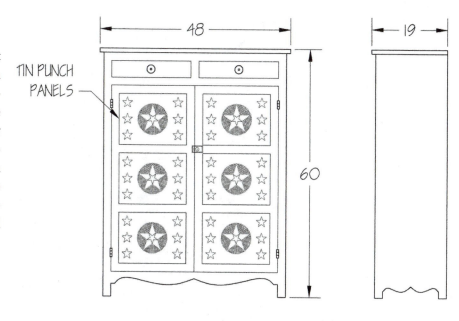

PIE SAFE (Pennsylvania Dutch Style)

SCALE - NTS

Fig. 6.32 A Pennsylvania Dutch–style pie safe with tin punched panels.

Chapter 6 Project and Quiz

Project 1

RESIDENTIAL DINING TABLE WITH LEAVES

Directions: Create two different dining table types, such as a standard table and trestle table.

Part 1: Create 5 to 10 thumbnail sketches in pencil or pen for each table.

Part 2: Design a dining table with leaves based on one of the two different styles shown in this chapter: standard leaf table or breadboard-style table. (The design can incorporate hand-carved pieces, but it should be based on a solid wood top.)

Part 3: Provide section and detail views of the table in part 2, and show the table with and without leaves.

Part 4: Provide a final color rendering.

Project 2

PEDESTAL DINING TABLE

Directions: Create a standard pedestal dining table.

Part 1: Create 5 to 10 thumbnail sketches in pencil or pen to create the basic idea of a pedestal table.

Part 2: Design a pedestal table with a veneer-style wood top. (The design can incorporate inlays as well as hand-carved pieces.)

Part 3: Provide section and detail views of the table showing how the pedestal is constructed.

Part 4: Provide a final color rendering.

Project 3

DINING CHAIRS

Directions: Create dining chairs.

Part 1: Create 5 to 10 thumbnail sketches of dining chairs based on the style of one of the tables in Project 1 or 2.

Part 2: Create both an armchair and a side chair from a front and side view.

Part 3: Create a section view of one of the chairs, showing the construction.

Part 4: Provide a final color rendering of one of the chairs.

Quiz

Directions: Circle the best answer choice for each of the following questions.

1. Which dimension is correct for a dining table height?
   A. 30"   B. 32"   C. 36"

2. What is used to attach the top of a dining table to the base?
   A. glue   B. nails   C. screws

3. Which dimension is correct for a dining chair seat height?
   A. 12"   B. 18"   C. 24"

4. Which dimension is correct for a dining chair seat depth?
   A. 12"   B. 16"   C. 20"

5. Which angle is correct for a dining chair seat back?
   A. 0°   B. 10°   C. 20°

6. Which of the following pieces will not be glued in door construction?
   A. rail   B. stile   C. panel

7. What type of concealed hinge should be used if the door fits inside of the frame?
   A. inset   B. overlay   C. half-overlay

8. Which of the following would be a low-end seat?
   A. drop in   B. webbed   C. spring

9. Which of the following would be a high-end seat?
   A. spring   B. zigzag   C. drop in

10. What do a bead, ogee, and radius refer to?
    A. upholstery
    B. door design
    C. hardware design

CHAPTER 7

Bedroom Furniture Design

THIS CHAPTER DISCUSSES how to design furniture for the bedroom. It starts with the most important piece of furniture—the bed—and lists basic mattress sizes from crib to California king and then explains how to design around these sizes while creating enough space for the bedding material. It also shows how to create drawings and details for the headboard, footboard, side rails, and stringers, as well as the types of materials used. It also includes information about a four-poster bed, a typical headboard and footboard bed, a platform bed, and a historic rope bed—to show how beds were made in the past. We also discuss how to design and construct a trundle bed as well as a hotel headboard that uses a cleat system.

The section on nightstands explains that the design of the nightstand is based on the dimensions of the bed design. This section illustrates basic drawer construction, reviews joinery for the drawer, and shows types of materials, material thickness, and function.

Next, different types of dressers are discussed, along with their basic dimensions. The section also explains the construction of a dresser and a chest of drawers, while illustrating modular design that uses many of the same parts over again.

The armoire and TV lift designs show how furniture is created as functional entertainment centers that also interact with technology. This section also shows how to design large pieces of furniture and explains hardware applications such as pocket doors and integrated lighting.

Finally, the chapter describes how to determine dimensions based on material sizes, such as plywood dimensions for an armoire, and how to incorporate efficient material use into your design.

Bed

A bed has four visible parts: a headboard, a footboard, and two rails. It also has an unseen part, the stringer system or bed slots, which support the box spring and/or mattress.

To design a bed you need to start with the mattress size and design the parts around that size. Table 7.1 gives standard mattress sizes. As a basic rule, you should leave a minimum of 1 inch of space all the way around the mattress from the rails, headboard, and footboard in order to fit the bedding materials on the mattress.

A typical bed will have four corners that come in contact with the floor and support the weight of the mattress. Two of these posts or legs are part of the headboard and two are part of the footboard. They are connected to

Table 7.1
Standard Mattress Sizes

Mattress Size	Width	Length
Crib	28″	52″
Twin (single)	39″	75″
Trundle (same as twin size)	39″	75″
Twin extra-long	39″	80″
Full (double)	54″	75″
Queen	60″	80″
King (standard or eastern)	76″	80″
California king (cal king)	72″	84″

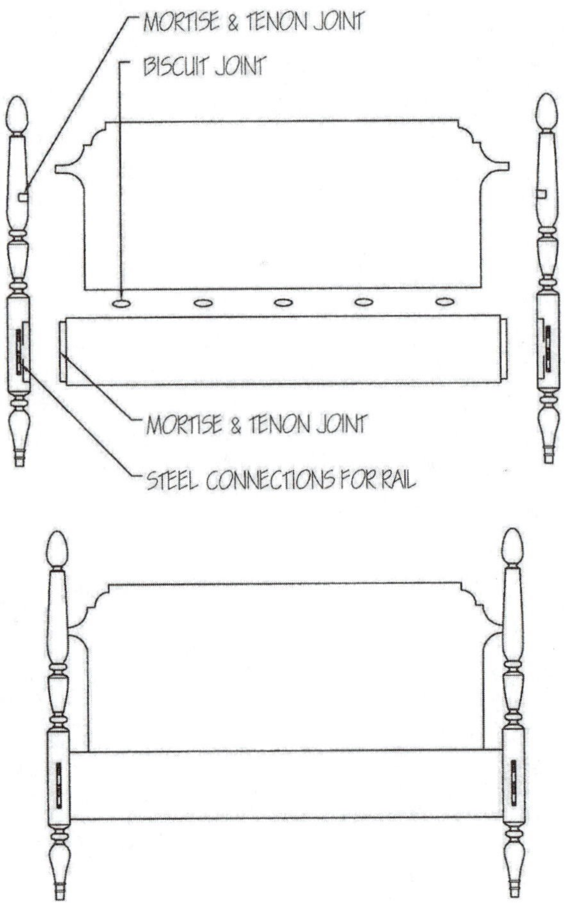

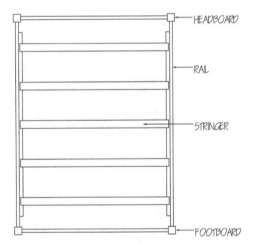

Fig. 7.1a A typical headboard construction exploded and assembled.

one rail on each side, typically using a mortise-and-tenon joint. (See Figure 7.1a.) The rest of the bed is connected to these pieces and is suspended, but these posts structurally support the weight of bedding.

The rails connect the footboard and the headboard and support the stringers. (See Figure 7.1b.) In order to prevent bowing of the rails, they should be at least 1¼ inch thick and 6 inches wide. Their length depends on the mattress. They need to connect to the footboard and headboard in a quick and easy fashion so that the bed can be disassembled to fit through a doorway, hallway, and so on. Special bed rail hardware is available for this purpose; it is

Fig. 7.1b A plan view of a typical bed with parts labeled.

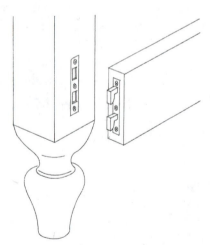

Fig. 7.1c Isometric view showing rail and headboard/footboard assembly.

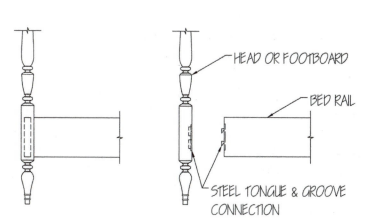

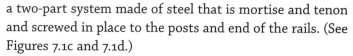

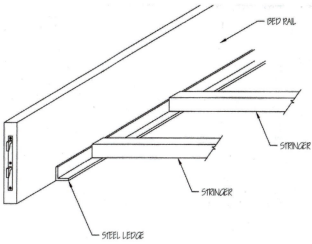

Fig. 7.1d Elevation view showing rail and headboard/footboard assembly.

Fig. 7.1e An isometric of a rail and stringer.

a two-part system made of steel that is mortise and tenon and screwed in place to the posts and end of the rails. (See Figures 7.1c and 7.1d.)

The stringers or bed slots connect both rails and support the box spring and mattress. Stringers are typically wood and should measure 1½ inches by 3 inches minimum; four or five stringers typically are used, depending on the size of the bed. The stringers sit on a ledge or cleat attached to the inside of the rails. A ledge is created with wood or steel and starts 3 to 4 inches from the end of the rail and runs the rest of its length. (See Figures 7.1e and 7.1f.)

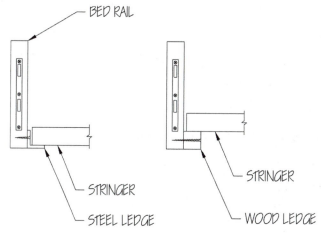

Fig. 7.1f A section view of a rail.

Headboard and Footboard

The headboard and footboard are typically constructed in the same way and should be designed to complement one another. The headboard is usually taller than the footboard and has two legs that are structural. These legs should have a minimum measurement of around 2 inches wide and 1½ inches thick; their height depends on the design. If the legs are turned pieces, they would start with a minimal square dimension of 2 inches by 2 inches. There is at least one structural piece to connect the two legs. This

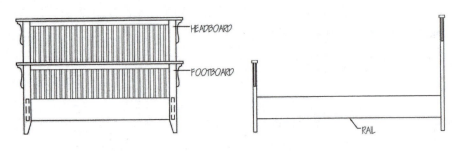

Fig. 7.2a Example of an orthographic Arts and Crafts–style bed.

Fig. 7.2b Elevation of headboard and footboard.

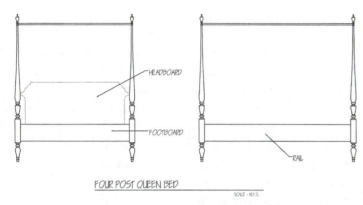

Fig. 7.3a Example of an orthographic four-post-style bed.

member is usually at the same height from the floor as the rails. The footboard's overall height is sometimes dictated by the placement of a TV in the bedroom. Figures 7.2a and 7.2b and Figures 7.3a and 7.3b show some examples of bed designs and construction.

With any four-poster bed that has a canopy, the canopy needs to break down into smaller parts for transportation, as does the rest of the bed. The design in Figure 7.3b shows a lap joint at the corners where the finial locks everything together.

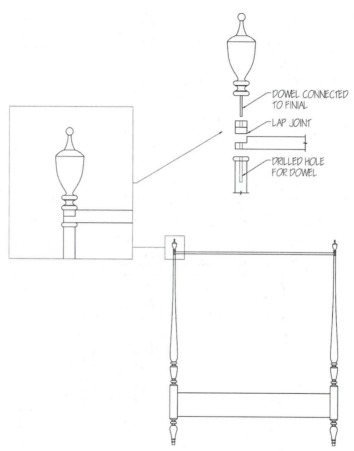

Fig. 7.3b Detail view of top finial from a four-poster bed.

UPHOLSTERED HEADBOARD

When upholstering a headboard, it is important to design the piece so that the upholstered part can be removed from the frame. This makes it possible to stain and finish the headboard frame and then attach the upholstery from behind. One way to do this is to use ¾-inch plywood as the backer board and then apply the desired thickness of foam with a top layer of batting material. The fabric or leather material is then wrapped around the foam-covered plywood and stapled to the back side of the plywood. To create a clean fit and finish for the headboard, the upholstered panel fits into a rabbet joint running along the back and finished from behind with a piece of ¼-inch plywood. This ¼-inch panel is then screwed to the headboard

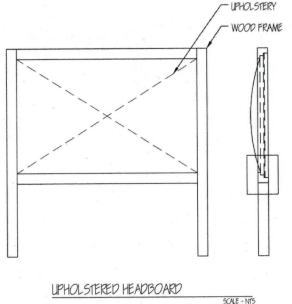

Fig. 7.4a An upholstered headboard with section detail.

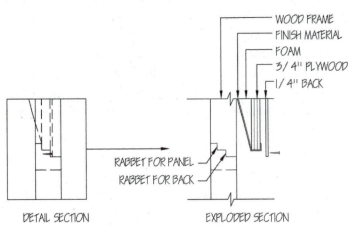

Fig. 7.4b An upholstered detail with exploded section detail.

without glue. This allows the upholstery to be removed for repair, reupholstery, or cleaning. (See Figures 7.4a and 7.4b.)

Platform Bed

A platform bed is constructed differently from a standard bed. The typical four legs with a headboard and footboard are replaced with a platform structure on which the mattress is placed. This structure can be made up of two basic parts, the base and the platform. Using a box spring is optional for platform beds, and with most contemporary designs it is not used, so the bed has a lower overall height. Some companies create a platform that has a wood bow frame inside that the mattress sits on, which creates the same effect as a box spring. (See Figure 7.5.)

Daybed

A daybed uses a twin (single) mattress (39″ × 75″) and is designed to function as a bed at night and sofa during the day. They are typically used in guest rooms or small spaces. The daybed is designed so that the length (75″) is positioned against the wall. The back and sides frame the mattress, and pillows add cushion to the back.

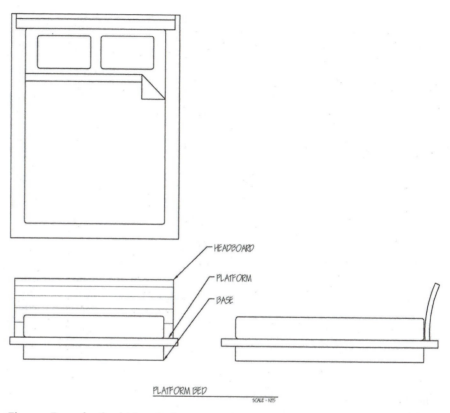

HEADBOARD

PLATFORM

BASE

PLATFORM BED

SCALE - NTS

Fig. 7.5 Example of a platform bed.

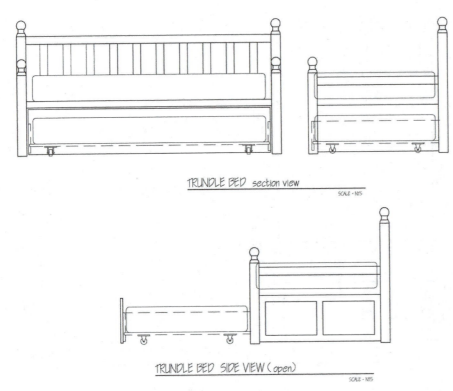

TRUNDLE BED section view

SCALE · NTS

TRUNDLE BED SIDE VIEW (open)

SCALE · NTS

Fig. 7.6 This example of a trundle bed shows the front and side views, with the third image showing the bottom mattress pulled out.

Trundle Bed

A trundle bed is basically a daybed with a hidden bed underneath. (See Figure 7.6.) The trundle uses the same size mattress as the daybed, a twin (single) that measures 39 inches by 75 inches. This size allows the bed to be used in a smaller room but still have the ability to expand to sleep two persons. A trundle bed is a good option for a child's room or guest room. Also, because it uses a bed mattress, it is more comfortable than a pull-out sleeper sofa. The trundle bed can be custom built, or special hardware is available to turn a daybed into a trundle, depending on how much negative space is available under the daybed and the height of the trundle mattress.

Commercial Headboard

In a hotel room the headboard is attached to the wall and not to the bed frame. This is done with a cleat system, where one cleat is screwed to the back of the headboard and another is screwed to the wall. Cleats are made of stamped metal or wood and run almost the length of the headboard. The examples in Figures 7.7a and 7.7b show a wood cleat that is ¾ inch thick with a 30 to 45-degree cut along one edge. This angled cut allows the headboard's

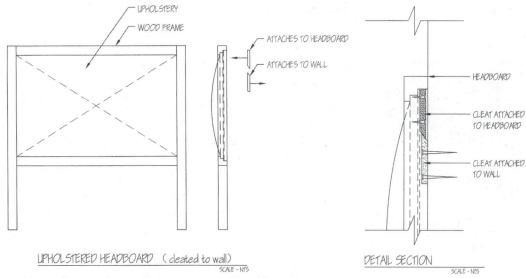

UPHOLSTERY
WOOD FRAME
ATTACHES TO HEADBOARD
ATTACHES TO WALL

UPHOLSTERED HEADBOARD (cleated to wall)
SCALE - NTS

HEADBOARD
CLEAT ATTACHED TO HEADBOARD
CLEAT ATTACHED TO WALL

DETAIL SECTION
SCALE - NTS

Fig. 7.7a Front and side views of a headboard with cleats.

Fig. 7.7b Example detail of the cleat system on a hotel headboard.

weight to secure it to the wall. Another type of hardware used to hold a headboard is the Z-clip, which works by mounting part of the clip to the back of the headboard (one on each end) and mounting the other half of the clip to the wall. The clips mounted to the wall need to be the same distance apart as the clips on the headboard. The headboard is then connected to the clips on the wall.

Fig. 7.8a Example of a historic rope bed.

Antique Beds

You can still find old beds in antique shops; they generally date from the 1700s to the 1900s. Many antique beds, like a rope bed, are also known as *three-quarter beds*. Antique bed frames are smaller than typical beds made today and therefore require a custom mattress and custom sheets. A rope bed supports the mattress by using a rope structure that is strung around pegs or through holes in the headboard, footboard, and rails. (See Figures 7.8a and 7.8b.) These ropes must be tightened from time to time to prevent the mattress from sagging. This is where the saying "sleep tight" comes from.

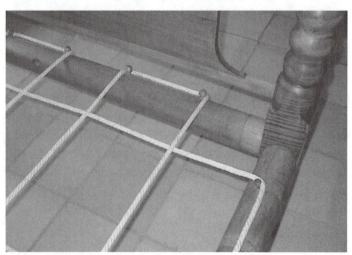

Fig. 7.8b Detail of a historic rope bed.

Nightstand

The function of a nightstand can vary from storage to display or both. No matter what the design, all nightstands have one thing in common: creating a surface area next to the bed. (See Figure 7.9.) Therefore, the bed's dimension and style usually affects the design of the nightstand. The top height of the nightstand is determined by the height of the top of the mattress from the floor. For example, a platform bed, which is lower to the floor than a standard bed, will typically have a lower nightstand.

Figure 7.9 Example of a nightstand

Drawers can be designed into the nightstand and can be constructed in many different ways. One way is to create a drawer box as a complete four-sided structure and then add a finished face to the structure. This means the interior drawer box walls are all connected together with a bottom floor as one complete unit. (See Figure 7.10.) The side walls are typically made of ½-inch-thick material with a ¼-inch-thick floor. The side walls are usually dovetailed or rabbet jointed together. The bottom (floor of the drawer) will float in a dado along the side wall.

Another construction style uses three sides with the drawer face making up the fourth side. (See Figure 7.11.) The construction of the box is the same as the first method, except for the front drawer face. The sides and the floor fit into a dado in the back of the drawer face. This is a good method to use if the front of the drawer face is curved.

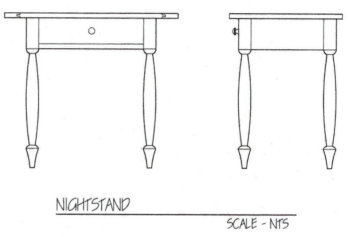

NIGHTSTAND

SCALE - NTS

Fig. 7.9 Example of a nightstand.

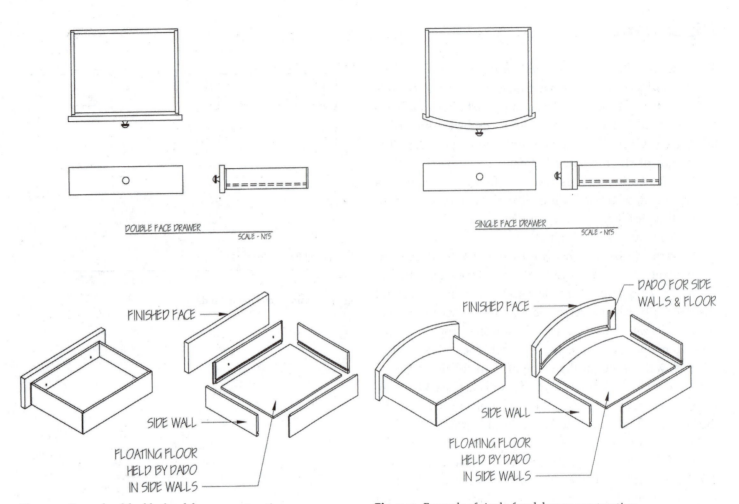

DOUBLE FACE DRAWER
SCALE - NTS

SINGLE FACE DRAWER
SCALE - NTS

FINISHED FACE

SIDE WALL

FLOATING FLOOR
HELD BY DADO
IN SIDE WALLS

DADO FOR SIDE
WALLS & FLOOR

FINISHED FACE

SIDE WALL

FLOATING FLOOR
HELD BY DADO
IN SIDE WALLS

Fig. 7.10 Example of double-faced drawer construction.

Fig. 7.11 Example of single-faced drawer construction.

The overhang from the drawer face to the interior box can vary depending on the type of drawer slide used. A typical overhang for side-mount metal slides is ½ inch on each side. (See Figure 7.12.) This allows the metal slide to be attached to the side of the drawer and the interior wall of the nightstand or dresser so that the drawer moves easily.

Typical side-mount drawer-slide hardware is available in two different styles. One is a standard kitchen cabinet style in which the drawer slides on a plastic roller. (See Figure 7.13a.) This type is used on lower-end furniture such as RTA (ready-to-assemble) furniture. The other style is a full-extension slide where the slide rolls on steel ball bearings, which create a smoother feel to the drawer as well as allowing the drawer to fully extend out from the cabinet. (See Figure 7.13b.) Both styles of drawer slides start at 10 inches long for shorter drawers and increase in size by 2 inch increments up to about 24 inches, depending on the manufacturer. Therefore, when designing the drawer, the depth is 1 to 2 inches longer than the metal slide.

When designing the drawer for any piece of furniture, the drawer box should not extend completely to the back of the inside of the cabinet. There should be a gap at the back of the drawer to the inside of the cabinet so that the inside of the drawer box does not hit the back of the cabinet. The recommended space is approximately 2 inches.

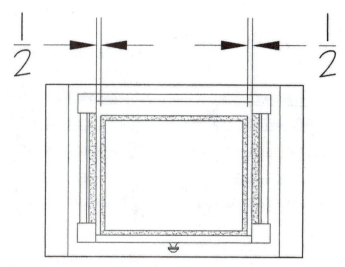

Fig. 7.12 Example of drawer gap tolerance for side-mount drawer slides; shaded areas are the interior side walls of the nightstand and the walls of the drawer box.

Fig. 7.13a A typical kitchen-cabinet-style drawer slide.

Fig. 7.13b A typical ball-bearing full-extension drawer slide.

Dresser and Chest of Drawers

A bedroom set typically comes with the following pieces: a bed, two nightstands, TV armoire or TV lift, and a dresser and/or chest of drawers. The difference between a dresser and a chest of drawers is the configuration of the drawers. A dresser is lower and wider with the drawers both stacked and next to one another; a chest of drawers is a taller piece of furniture that has the drawers stacked vertically. (See Figure 7.14a.) A basic dresser and a chest of drawers are constructed in the same way. (See Figures 7.14b through f.)

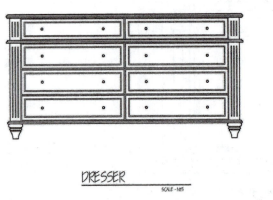

DRESSER
SCALE - NTS

CHEST OF DRAWERS
SCALE - NTS

Fig. 7.14a Examples of a dresser and a chest of drawers.

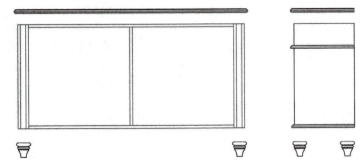

Fig. 7.14b A breakdown of the structural case of a dresser.

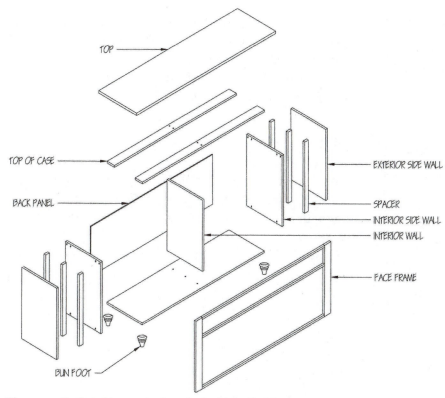

TOP

TOP OF CASE

BACK PANEL

EXTERIOR SIDE WALL

SPACER

INTERIOR SIDE WALL

INTERIOR WALL

FACE FRAME

BUN FOOT

Fig. 7.14c Exploded isometric view of a double-walled dresser.

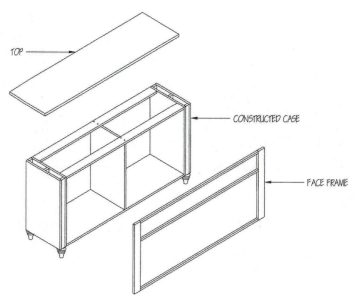

TOP

CONSTRUCTED CASE

FACE FRAME

Fig. 7.14d Isometric view of constructed case with face frame and top.

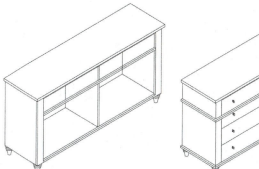

Fig. 7.14e Isometric view of completed case without drawers.

Fig. 7.14f Complete isometric view of dresser.

161

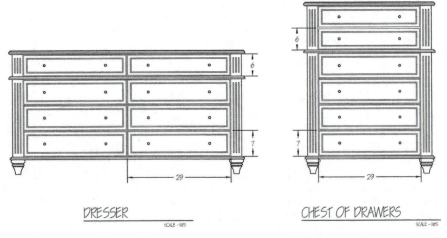

DRESSER

CHEST OF DRAWERS

SCALE - NTS   SCALE - NTS

Fig. 7.15a Modular production with the drawer design: each dresser uses the same size smaller and larger drawer.

With production furniture it is common for the manufacturer to use the same drawer size for both the dresser and the chest of drawers to cut down on costs. Manufacturers also often use standard sizes among different design styles. (See Figure 7.15a.)

Highboy

The highboy is a chest-on-chest design that is generally 7 feet tall or taller. The bottom chest is designed like a lowboy with long legs and drawers. The top chest typically has

HIGHBOY

Fig. 7.15b The front and side elevation of a highboy.

drawers stacked to the top. These top drawers sometimes can be reached only by using a chair or stool. For this reason highboys are not found in typical bedroom sets but are replaced by a dresser or a lower chest of drawers. (See Figure 7.15b.)

Armoire

The armoire began its history as a clothing wardrobe. Historically, it took the place of a home's closet, because at the time dwellings did not have closets. As the closet became a common part of bedrooms, the armoire became obsolete. Once the television was invented, however, the armoire was once again needed; now its function is to hide the TV and not clothing. As TVs grew larger, so have armoires. However, the need for this piece will probably disappear again as TVs become flatter and thinner. TVs can now be hung on the wall like a picture or can be hidden in a lift system (discussed later in this chapter).

Because the armoire is a large item and needs to support a lot of weight, it is engineered differently from other bedroom furniture. One way to design a piece to support more weight is to construct a double wall, as shown in the dresser designs in Figures 7.14b through f. The double wall provides a double thickness for the outside structure of the piece. This adds strength to the overall piece both vertically and horizontally. (See Figures 7.16a and b; 7.17a through d; and 7.18.) The outside walls are connected by a bottom floor and a top. Depending on the design, a center shelf can also connect the walls to provide added strength. The inside of an armoire is made from a veneer

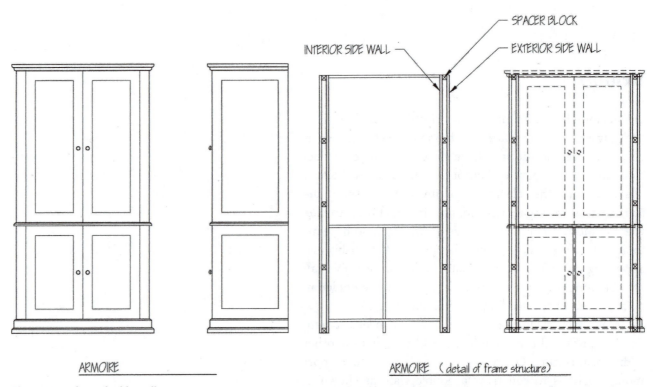

ARMOIRE

Fig. 7.16a A basic double-wall armoire.

ARMOIRE (detail of frame structure)

Fig. 7.16b A basic double-wall structure. Inside walls are ¾″ thick plywood; outside walls are ¾″ thick plywood with a 1½″ spacer between the walls. There is also a center ¾″ plywood vertical piece to support the weight of the TV.

Fig. 7.17a The plywood case of a double-wall armoire.

Fig. 7.17b The case with face frame.

Fig. 7.17c Base and crown molding added with a TV shelf.

Fig. 7.17d Interior with pocket doors open and a bottom shelf.

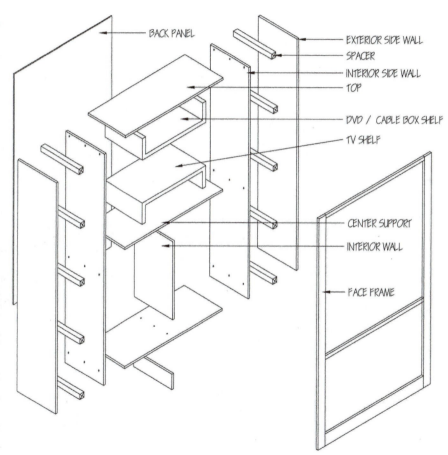

BACK PANEL

EXTERIOR SIDE WALL

SPACER

INTERIOR SIDE WALL

TOP

DVD / CABLE BOX SHELF

TV SHELF

CENTER SUPPORT

INTERIOR WALL

FACE FRAME

Fig. 7.18 Exploded isometric view showing the basic case structure of a double-wall armoire.

core plywood, and the depth is typically 24 inches. This is enough space to hold a standard TV while using the plywood material efficiently. Plywood's standard size is 48 inches by 96 inches; therefore, one sheet of plywood will make both inside walls when cut in half.

One added detail an armoire can have is pocket doors. Pocket doors open like typical doors and then can slide back into the armoire, exposing the TV for easy viewing. There are some restrictions to these doors, however. The first is that the design typically needs to use inset doors because pocket door hardware is basically a concealed inset hinge mounted to a drawer slide. Both the top and bottom slides are connected by either a cable system or

Fig. 7.19a Pocket door pulled out.   **Fig. 7.19b** Pocket door pushed in.

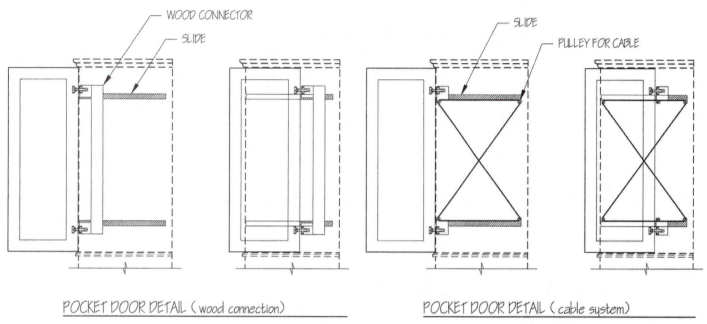

WOOD CONNECTOR

SLIDE

SLIDE

PULLEY FOR CABLE

POCKET DOOR DETAIL (wood connection)

POCKET DOOR DETAIL (cable system)

Fig. 7.20a The pocket door open. The wood connector allows the door slides to work as one complete unit.

Fig. 7.20b The pocket door slid into the armoire. The cable system runs on a pulley system that distributes the door weight evenly.

a connecting piece of wood. This allows the door to slide cleanly into the armoire. (See Figures 7.19a and 7.19b and 7.20a and 7.20b.)

Because the pocket door takes up space inside the armoire, the TV cannot completely fill the interior space. As a general rule, the designer should leave 3 inches between each side of the TV and the inside walls of the armoire. (See Figure 7.21.) This will leave enough space for

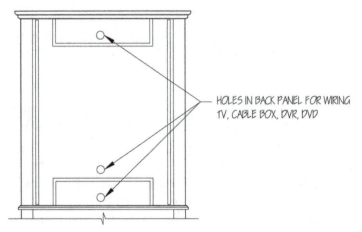

ARMOIRE

Fig. 7.21 A spacing of 3″ from inside wall to side of TV will allow enough space for the pocket door and pocket door hardware.

the pocket door hardware and door thickness to fit inside while not interfering with the TV.

Other items that need to be designed into the armoire are spacing for a cable box, DVD player, DVR, and any other electronic equipment. These items can be placed on shelves inside the armoire, but because the pocket door slides into the interior space the shelves need to be mounted to either the ceiling or the center shelf of the armoire. Also, holes need to be drilled in the back wall for the wiring of these items. Typically, a 2-inch-diameter hole allows all of the plugs and cables to fit. (See Figure 7.22.) The back panel is typically ¼ inch thick; slots should be cut into the back wall behind the TV to ensure proper venting of heat from all of the electronic equipment.

HOLES IN BACK PANEL FOR WIRING TV, CABLE BOX, DVR, DVD

Fig. 7.22 Typical placement of holes in a back panel for wiring purpose.

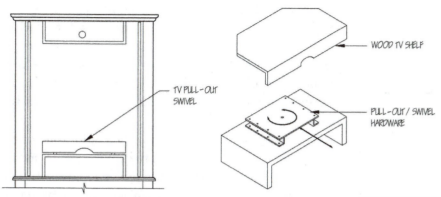

Fig. 7.23 A TV pull-out; note the corners are notched on the shelf to prevent damage to the inside of door when the shelf is turned.

For a hotel armoire, some other items may need to be configured into the design. The first is a pull-out TV swivel, which is also popular in residential armoires. This item allows the TV to be pulled out from the armoire and to swivel about 30 degrees in each direction. (See Figure 7.23.) The hardware for this is basically a heavy-duty slide mounted to a swivel. The hardware is screwed and bolted to the armoire's center shelf that supports the TV. Then a wood shelf is screwed to the top of the swivel. The TV sits on this shelf, which covers the pull-out hardware.

Another item that may be included in a hotel armoire is a mini bar. (See Figure 7.24.) The main concern for a mini bar is that there is adequate venting in the back of the armoire to prevent the mini refrigerator from overheating. Venting slits can be cut into the back of the piece, but the

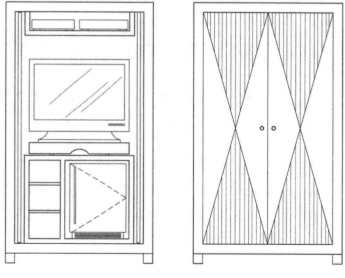

HOTEL ARMOIRE / MINI BAR

Fig. 7.24 A hotel-style armoire with space for a mini bar and adjustable shelves below.

ARMOIRE

Fig. 7.25 A two-piece highboy-style armoire. The two pieces are disguised by the center molding.

armoire should not be installed flush to the wall. A 1- to 2-inch gap needs to exist between the wall and the back of the armoire for proper venting. The manufacturer of the mini refrigerator will specify how much space is needed. The other detail that needs to be addressed is to ensure that the doors of the armoire do not interfere with the door of the mini refrigerator.

Some other basic styles of armoires are the highboy armoire, bonnet-top armoire, and full-length-door armoire. The highboy armoire, shown in Figure 7.25, is an armoire with longer legs and typically two pieces stacked on top of each other. This is styled after the highboy dresser of the sixteenth century. The bonnet-top armoire is an armoire with a curved top. (See Figure 7.26.) A full-length-door armoire can be designed as a wardrobe or as an entertainment center. If it will house a TV, then it must be designed with an interior structure to hold the TV so that the doors can slide into the interior of the piece. (See Figure 7.27.) Any interior drawers need to be designed to leave enough space for the doors to close; therefore, the armoire's depth needs to take door thickness and knob dimension into consideration.

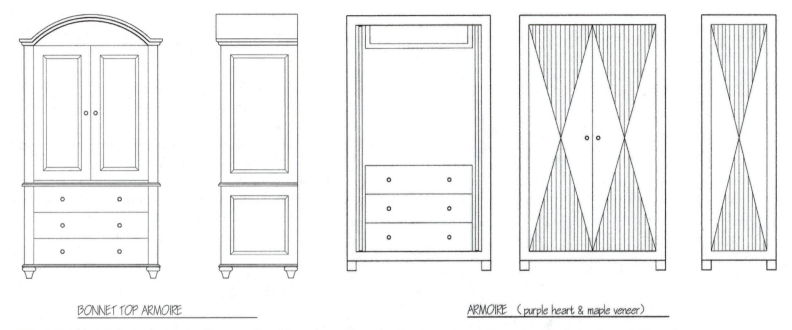

BONNET TOP ARMOIRE

ARMOIRE (purple heart & maple veneer)

Fig. 7.26 A bonnet-top-style armoire. The curved top can be created with bender board and finished with veneer.

Fig. 7.27 A contemporary-style armoire. This design shows full-length veneered doors with a hidden drawer system inside.

TV Lift

The TV lift, also known as a TV pop-up, is a fairly new type of furniture. It accomplishes the same thing as an armoire by hiding the TV, but it does so in a completely different way. It is simply a box with a lift mechanism that can raise, lower, and sometimes spin a TV. It lifts the TV for viewing and retracts it back into the piece so that it is out of sight. This piece of furniture did not become popular until the advent of the flat-screen TV, the size of which allows it to be incorporated into another piece like a dresser. The design is first based on the TV's size; from there the lift is chosen based on that TV. The companies that make these lifts provide specifications describing the size and weight that their product can lift. They also have different types of lifts for standard TVs and plasma-screen TVs.

Standard TV Lift

This type of design is basically an outside cabinet with a box that holds the TV, which is lifted up and down by a remote control. Once the TV and lift are chosen, the outside cabinet is built around the lift mechanism. Service doors need to be incorporated into the design. If the piece is placed against the wall, the service doors are on the front of the piece. If the piece is to be placed in front of the bed, the doors are on the back. These doors are for servicing

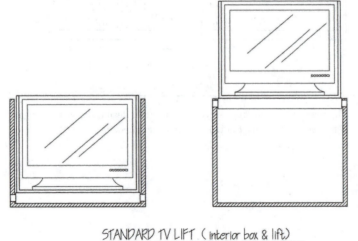

STANDARD TV LIFT (interior box & lift)

Fig. 7.28a A basic TV lift and interior box for a standard TV.

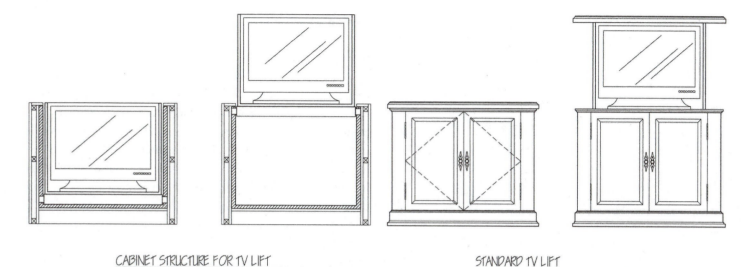

CABINET STRUCTURE FOR TV LIFT

Fig. 7.28b The cabinet structure; note that because of the weight of all items contained inside, it is recommended to design the exterior cabinet as a double-wall cabinet.

STANDARD TV LIFT

Fig. 7.28c The complete TV lift, also known as a TV pop-up.

the mechanism if it gets jammed or needs a fuse. The inside box holds the TV and includes a base (floor), two sides, and a back, which are all typically made from ¾-inch plywood. The top is a floating top that is not glued to the inside box. It is held in position with dowels. This is to protect users from getting their fingers pinched when the system is being closed. Also, any shelves are held in place by shelf pins rather than being glued to the inside box. (See Figures 7.28a to c.)

Flat-Screen Lift

A plasma-screen or LCD flat-screen lift can lift the TV in the same way as a standard TV lift, or it can use a different design where the TV is mounted from the back, basically hanging the TV in the same way it would be if it were mounted to a wall. The best part of this design is that a flat-screen TV does not take up much space, so it can be incorporated into a dresser design. A typical dresser is 18 inches deep, and a TV pop-up dresser is typically 24 inches deep with shallow drawers that create space for the TV and the lift. This cuts down on the total number of pieces in the space.

The lift mechanism is mounted to a solid surface. Typically, it mounts to the floor of the cabinet and has a telescoping tube that lifts the TV. Other mechanisms mount to the back of the cabinet, so instead of using ¼-inch material for the back, this design requires ¾-inch material for the lift to be mounted to. The top of the lift can either be hinged to the back of the dresser and swing back when the TV is lifted or come with a mounting bracket for the top of the dresser. (See Figures 7.29a to c.)

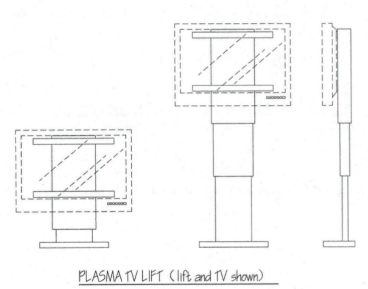

PLASMA TV LIFT (lift and TV shown)

Fig. 7.29a A flat-screen TV lift; note that the TV mounts from the back.

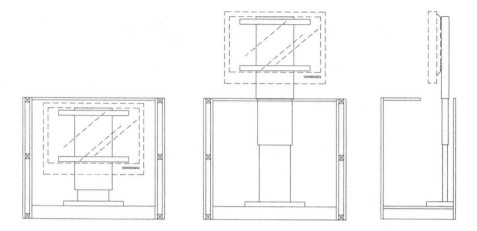

CABINET STRUCTURE FOR TV LIFT

Fig. 7.29b The cabinet structure for a dresser-style plasma-screen TV pop-up.

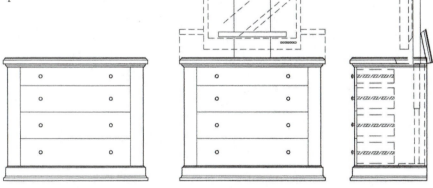

PLASMA TV LIFT (dresser with 4 drawers)

Fig. 7.29c A dresser-style flat-screen TV pop-up; note that it is deeper than a typical dresser.

Chapter 7 Project and Quiz

Project 1

MODULAR DESIGN: BEDROOM SET

Directions: Create two different sets of bedroom furniture (one design must have historical influence). Each set should use the same basic modular parts. The pieces must reuse the same elements (e.g., case, drawers, doors) as shown in this chapter.

Part 1: Concept page: Type a brief description of the style that your design is influenced by and include the date or time span and a photo of that style.

Part 2: AutoCAD or manually draft an orthographic projection in ¾-inch or 1-inch scale of all of the following items in two different design ideas:

A. one bed
B. one nightstand
C. one dresser
D. one chest of drawers

Part 3: Marker rendering: Reprint one orthographic projection piece and render all views showing material surfaces, highlights, and shadows.

Project 2

TV LIFT

Directions: Create a TV pop-up in any style and show all correct details. Provide a specification sheet of the motorized TV lift. Keep in mind that the drawing must be based around the TV size.

Part 1: Create 5 to 10 thumbnail sketches in pencil or pen to illustrate your basic idea.

Part 2: Show the TV pop-up in orthographic projection with the lift down; label and show dimensions. (See Figure 7.30a.)

Part 3: Show the TV pop-up in orthographic projection with the lift up; label and show dimensions. (See Figure 7.30b.)

Part 4: Provide a color rendering in elevation view.

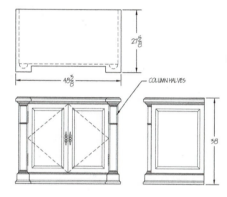

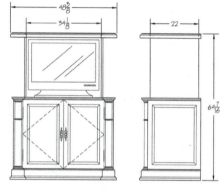

Fig. 7.30a Example of TV pop-up in orthographic projection with the lift down, including labels and dimensions.

Fig. 7.30b Example of TV pop-up in orthographic projection with the lift up, including labels and dimensions.

Quiz

Directions: Circle the best answer choice for each of the following questions.

1. What is the size of a trundle mattress?
   A. 39" × 75"   B. 39" × 80"   C. 54" × 75"

2. What is the size of a king mattress?
   A. 70" × 80"   B. 76" × 80"   C. 76" × 84"

3. What should be the minimum bed rail thickness?
    A. 1" B. 1¼" C. 1½"

4. What does a cleat allow the headboard to do?
    A. attach to the wall
    B. attach to the rails
    C. attach to a nightstand

5. A trundle bed will have which of the following?
    A. a platform as a base
    B. a pull-out bed under the top mattress
    C. ropes instead of a box spring

6. Which of the following is a typical joint for drawer construction?
    A. tongue and groove
    B. mortise and tenon
    C. dovetail

7. What gap is needed for side-mount drawer slides?
    A. ½" on each side
    B. ¾" on each side
    C. 1" on each side

8. What is the dimensional space needed for a pocket door to slide into an armoire?
    A. 1" B. 3" C. 5"

9. What are pocket doors?
    A. overlay doors
    B. inset doors
    C. half-overlay doors

10. If a TV lift is designed to fit in front of a footboard,
    where are the access doors located?
        A. front   B. sides   C. back

Living Room Furniture Design

THIS CHAPTER ILLUSTRATES the different pieces found in a living room or great room, including the coffee table, end table, sofa table, entertainment center, and upholstered items. Basic dimensions are given for the different types of furniture and how these dimensions relate to one another. This chapter also discusses different materials and how materials can change depending on the desired function of the piece.

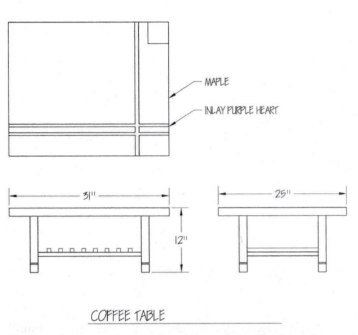

MAPLE

INLAY PURPLE HEART

31"

25"

12"

COFFEE TABLE

Fig. 8.1a Orthographic view of a rectilinear-designed coffee table.

Fig. 8.1b The final piece made in maple and purple heart with inlay.

Coffee Table

The coffee table is generally positioned in front of a sofa or love seat; therefore, its dimensions need to complement the sofa's seat height. The basic dimensions for the coffee table to be functional are 16 inches wide, 36 inches long, and 12 to 18 inches tall. These dimensions vary based on the design of the piece, size of the sofa, and size of the room.

The coffee table is typically used for holding books and magazines as well as drinks while watching TV or visiting with guests; therefore, coaster sets can be displayed to protect the finish. (See Figures 8.1a and 8.1b.) Storage can be added to this piece by adding a drawer under the top surface or by changing it into a trunk for larger storage. A drawback of a trunk design is that any items sitting on top of the table need to be removed in order to open the piece, as shown in Figure 8.2.

The coffee table can provide a strong statement about a room's style because it is the centerpiece to the seating. The example in Figure 8.3 shows an Art Deco–style table. Figure 8.4 shows an orthographic drawing of a Louis XVI–inspired table. Orthographic drawings can provide additional details, such as where two different materials like the wood frame of the table and a stone insert top come together. Note that when measuring the size of the wood base for a stone or glass insert the top material should be $\frac{1}{16}$ inch smaller on all sides to ensure a good fit.

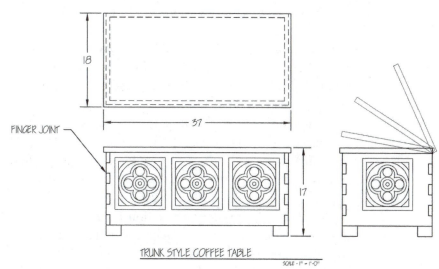

FINGER JOINT

TRUNK STYLE COFFEE TABLE
SCALE - 1" = 1'-0"

Fig. 8.2 A trunk designed for larger amounts of storage. The corners are connected with a finger joint.

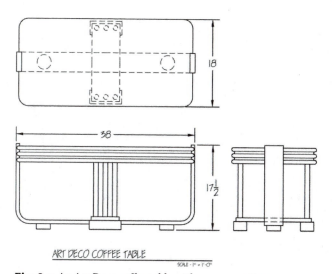

ART DECO COFFEE TABLE
SCALE - 1" = 1'-0"

Fig. 8.3 An Art Deco coffee table with open negative space below.

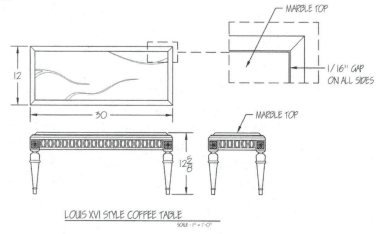

MARBLE TOP

1/16" GAP
ON ALL SIDES

MARBLE TOP

LOUIS XVI STYLE COFFEE TABLE
SCALE - 1" = 1'-0"

Fig. 8.4 A Louis XVI–inspired coffee table with a marble top.

End Table

The end table or small side table accents the ends of a sofa. The typical dimensions for this piece are 24 inches by 24 inches by 24 inches but can vary depending on the design of the end table and the size and scale of the sofa. The main function of this piece is to create a flat surface plane to the side(s) of the sofa. This piece can be designed for many functions, such as storage for books, magazines, and remote controls or as a surface to place lighting. (See Figure 8.5.)

The door and drawer construction for an end table is the same as for other pieces, such as the nightstand discussed in Chapter 7—in many ways an end table is very much like a nightstand. The main difference is that, depending on the room, the layout of the end table could be seen from all sides, whereas the nightstand is against a wall next to the bed.

The way to start designing this piece is to determine its function and style. Does it simply need to be a surface for a lamp? Does it need to have storage, and if so, what kind—drawers, doors, or both? What is the overall style of the room? Once these questions have been answered, you can start creating thumbnail sketches. Figures 8.6, 8.7, 8.8a, and 8.8b show some different examples of end table designs.

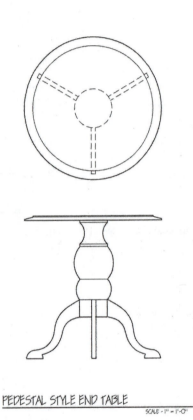

PEDESTAL STYLE END TABLE

SCALE - 1" = 1'-0"

Fig. 8.5 Pedestal side table without storage.

ARTS & CRAFTS STYLE END TABLE
SCALE - 1" = 1'-0"

Fig. 8.6 Arts and Crafts style with a drawer and lower fixed shelf.

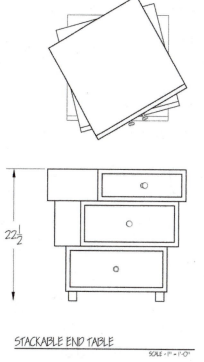

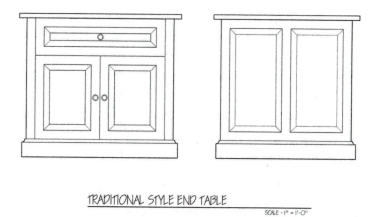

TRADITIONAL STYLE END TABLE
SCALE - 1" = 1'-0"

Fig. 8.7 Traditional style with a drawer and doors below for storage.

$22\frac{1}{2}$

STACKABLE END TABLE
SCALE - 1" = 1'-0"

Fig. 8.8a AutoCAD image of a modular-designed end table with three drawers.

Fig. 8.8b Final piece of the modular-designed end table.

Sofa Table

The sofa table is positioned behind the sofa and provides a functional top display surface. It can have drawers, doors, or shelving for extra display or storage. It is designed based on the sofa's dimensions so that the top of the table is at or slightly below the top of the sofa. This piece is typically narrow so that it does not interfere with the traffic flow of the room; 12 to 18 inches wide is a reasonable standard size. The total length is dictated by the sofa; the table should be at least 12 inches shorter than the sofa. (See Figures 8.9, 8.10, and 8.11.)

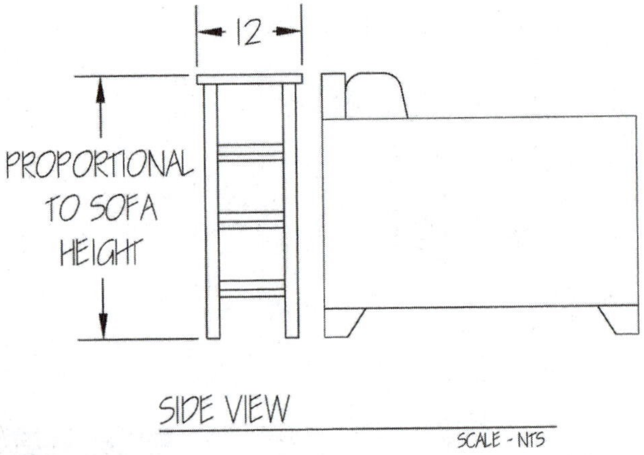

PROPORTIONAL TO SOFA HEIGHT

12

SIDE VIEW

SCALE - NTS

Fig. 8.9 The basic height and depth dimensions of a sofa table.

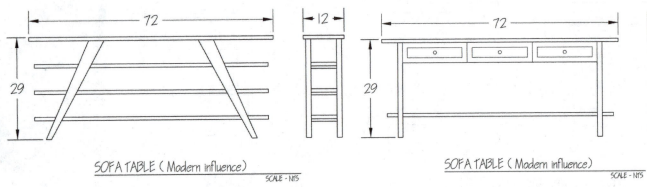

SOFA TABLE (Modern influence)

SCALE - NTS

72 12 29

Fig. 8.10 A contemporary sofa table with fixed shelves.

SOFA TABLE (Modern influence)

SCALE - NTS

72 16 29

Fig. 8.11 A contemporary sofa table with drawers and a fixed lower shelf.

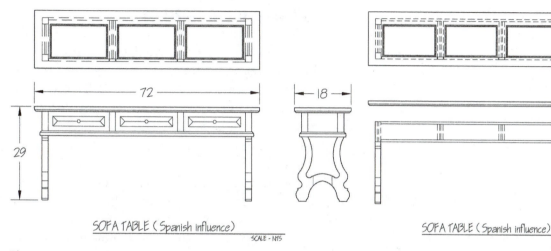

SOFA TABLE (Spanish influence)
SCALE - NTS

SOFA TABLE (Spanish influence)
SCALE - NTS

BISCUIT JOINT

Fig. 8.12a A Spanish-influenced sofa table with three drawers.

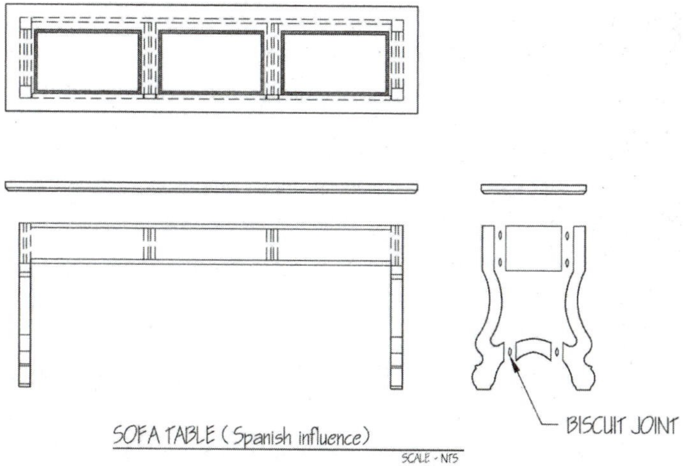

Fig. 8.12b Exploded elevation view of a sofa table.

The design of the piece and the function it is intended to fulfill determines how it is constructed. The piece in Figures 8.12a through c is a Spanish-influenced design with three drawers. The drawers fit into their own compartments, with the gap tolerance based on the type of drawer slide used. Figure 8.12c shows an exploded view of all the parts used to create the piece.

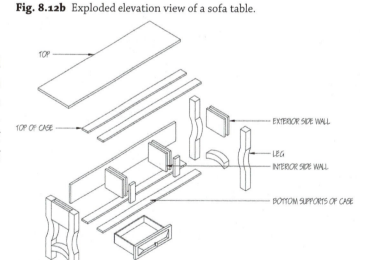

TOP

TOP OF CASE

EXTERIOR SIDE WALL

LEG

INTERIOR SIDE WALL

BOTTOM SUPPORTS OF CASE

Fig. 8.12c Exploded isometric view of a sofa table.

Entertainment Center

The entertainment center is similar to the armoire discussed in Chapter 7. The function of this piece is to hide electrical items, such as a TV, cable box, DVD player, and so on, and it can also serve as a storage area. The entertainment center is a large item, and large pieces need to designed and engineered to break apart to fit through doorways for delivery.

The entertainment center can be a freestanding piece like an armoire, or it can look like a built-in wall piece made from multiple components, creating a much larger item. The starting point for any entertainment center is to determine the overall dimensions of the desired electrical components that will be stored in the unit such as the TV, cable box, and so on. Note that the basic dimension normally given for a TV (e.g., a 36″ TV) is the diagonal screen measurement and not the TV's overall size. The dimension that is needed to create the entertainment center is the overall length, width, and height of the entire TV.

The next step is to determine how much storage the client needs and whether the piece will have open shelving for displaying items or doors to conceal them. Other considerations are the different electronic items to be housed inside the center and whether they need to be connected to each other. Consider the need for specialized storage features, such as DVDs and video games. The final consideration is the TV's height from the floor. This measurement is determined by the seating height in the room.

Armoire-Style Entertainment Center

The most popular entertainment center configuration is a vertical-style armoire. This piece has the TV placed slightly above center with drawers or doors below. Because this is a large piece, plywood is used to create the structure's case. Plywood is available in 4-feet-by-8-feet sheets; to maximize the material the board is cut in half to create two 24-inch panels. These panels are then cut down to the desired height so that one sheet can be used for both sides of the armoire. Once the face frame of solid wood is added, the side of the armoire will be 24¾ inches wide; armoires are typically 22½ inches to 24¾ inches deep, a dimension that represents just the size of the case. Once the applied molding (e.g., base molding or crown molding) is added, the armoire's overall size will increase. (See Figure 8.13.) Applied molding can be added to the sides to create the effect of panels and to add detail to the overall look of the piece. The molding is glued and nailed with small brad nails. The corners are mitered to create a complete uniform look to the molding. The face frame can also have detail added to it with a router, like the piece shown in Figure 8.13, to create an architectural fluting detail to the sides.

Another configuration is the horizontal-style armoire. This piece has the TV on one side and shelves on the other to hold the electrical components. (See Figure 8.14.) Typically, a third center foot is added to support the weight of the piece when loaded with items. Without this center foot

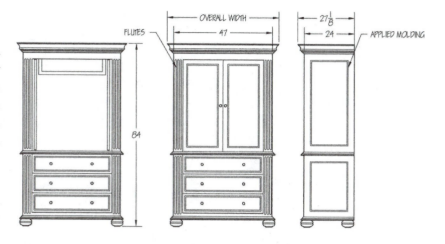

ARMOIRE STYLE (entertainment center)

Fig. 8.13 An armoire-style vertical configuration for an entertainment center. Note that applied molding has been added to the sides as well as flutes to the face frame.

ARMOIRE STYLE (entertainment center)

Fig. 8.14 Armoire-style horizontal configuration for an entertainment center.

the piece may begin to bow over time. One main drawback to this style is that it places the TV much lower to the ground, which can make it difficult to view in a large room where other furniture may be in the way. It also takes up more wall space horizontally, which can make it hard to place the piece in a room.

Wall Unit Entertainment Center

The wall unit entertainment center is made up of modular pieces, typically three, five, or more, particularly if the TV unit is combined with multiple library and storage display units. The center breaks down into pieces for transportation and delivery purposes. A typical doorway is usually 30 to 36 inches wide; therefore, the large piece needs to break down into smaller pieces that will fit through that size opening.

Modular items are held together with screws from the inside so that they are not visible. Most manufacturers supply non-tipping brackets to prevent larger, heavy casegoods from falling forward. The center piece is typically like a vertical-style armoire and holds the major electronic items. The side pieces are not as deep and have shelves, doors, or drawers for extra storage. Making the center piece 24 inches deep and the sides 20 inches deep, for example, will create a seamless connection between the parts. These side pieces can also hold speakers with a front cover so that they are not seen. (See Figures 8.15a and 8.15b.)

3 PIECE ENTERTAINMENT CENTER

Fig. 8.15a Three-piece wall unit entertainment center.

3 PIECE ENTERTAINMENT CENTER

Fig. 8.15b Individual pieces of an entertainment center, connected with screws.

Corner Cabinet Armoire

The corner cabinet armoire is a unique piece of furniture because it is designed to fit in the corner of a room. Although it seems simple enough to create—it is an armoire with the sides cut to a 45-degree angle—it is a little more complicated than that. The first thing to address is the total depth. If the far back of the piece makes a right-angled corner, the piece will be too deep to fit through a doorway.

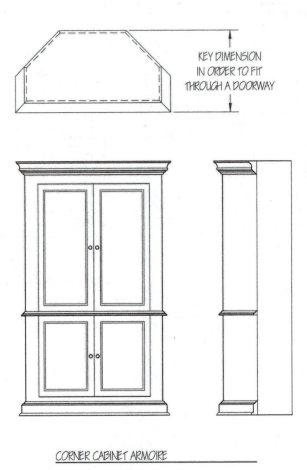

CORNER CABINET ARMOIRE

Fig. 8.16a A corner cabinet entertainment center. Note the total dimension of the depth needs to be smaller than the doorway opening in order for the piece to be delivered.

(See Figure 8.16a.) The back corner needs to be a flat panel that runs parallel to the front of the piece. This means that when the piece is installed it will not touch the corner of the wall but instead creates a small negative space.

The second characteristic that differentiates a corner cabinet is the drawers. Drawers on a corner cabinet do not maximize the total space because the drawers are at a right angle and the corner cabinet is not. Compared to the cabinet itself, each drawer needs to be smaller in width, which creates dead space to each side of the drawer, or smaller in total depth, which creates dead space behind the drawer. (See Figures 8.16b and 8.16c.)

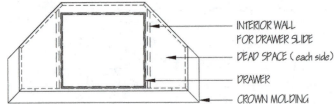

Fig. 8.16b Drawer detail when made to fit to the back of the cabinet.

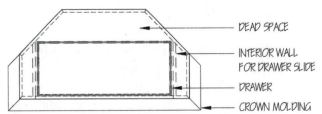

Fig. 8.16c Drawer detail with a shallow drawer.

Bifold Door

A bifold door has two sets of hinges, and the door is either split down the center or, more typically, uses two narrow doors. The hinge is a standard concealed or pin hinge that attaches to the outer door and the cabinet. The second door is connected to the first door with a special bifold hinge from the back side so that the hinge is not seen from the front. Two hinges are used for each door. Each hinge has a spring inside to make it easier to open the panels. (See Figures 8.17a and 8.17b.)

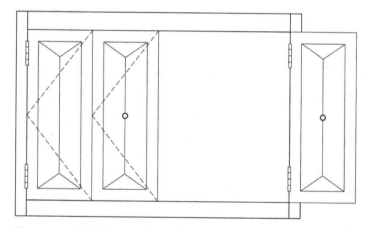

Fig. 8.17a A bifold door with one door open.

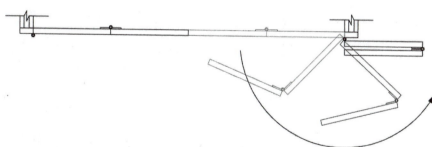

Fig. 8.17b Top view of bifold doors and how they open.

Giant-Screen TVs

When designing an entertainment center for a giant-screen TV, it is essential to design around the TV. These types of TVs are on hidden wheels so that they can be rolled into place. Therefore, the TV stays on the floor surface, and the armoire fits around it. When the piece is installed, the TV slides into its position and a front access panel is attached, typically with roller catches, so that it can be removed in order to service the TV. (See Figures 8.17c through e.)

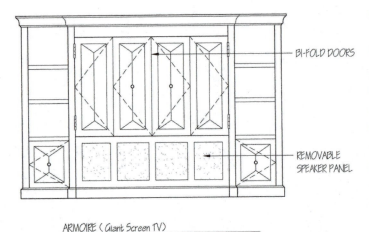

ARMOIRE (Giant Screen TV)

Fig. 8.17c Entertainment center designed for a giant-screen TV.

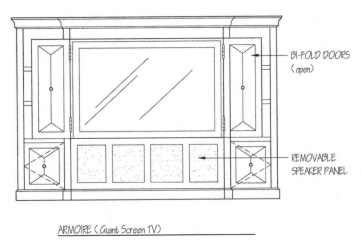

ARMOIRE (Giant Screen TV)

Fig. 8.17d The unit with bifold doors open.

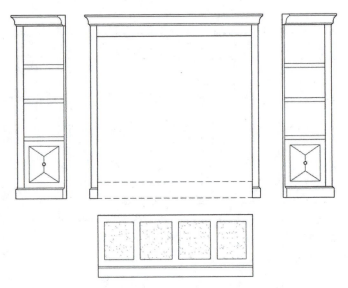

Fig. 8.17e The breakdown of complete case parts. The sides are connected with screws and the front speaker panel is connected with roller catches.

Sofa and Love Seat

An upholstered sofa or love seat can be broken down into a few different parts: frame, spring structure, cushion, and finish material. These different parts can change the total price of the piece, and because most of these parts are internal, clients needs to understand what they are paying for and how each part is constructed.

The frame should be constructed from a kiln-dried hardwood such as ash, birch, maple, oak, or poplar. Lower-end sofas will have a pine or Douglas fir frame, which are softwoods. A softwood frame is a weaker frame and will flex when weight is applied. Higher-end pieces use a double-cone spring for the seat area and either a double-cone or zigzag or sinuous wire spring for the back of the sofa; a lower-end sofa uses only webbing on the seat and back to support the cushions. Most cushions are foam with a layer of batting around the foam, which is covered by the finish material. Some cushions are spring cushions in which double-cone springs are covered by a thin layer of foam and batting, then the finished material. (See Figure 8.18.)

The drawings in Figures 8.19 and 8.20 show the basic dimensions for a sofa and a love seat. These dimensions can be altered based on the style and design of the piece.

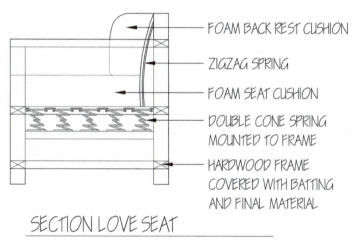

SECTION LOVE SEAT

FOAM BACK REST CUSHION

ZIGZAG SPRING

FOAM SEAT CUSHION

DOUBLE CONE SPRING MOUNTED TO FRAME

HARDWOOD FRAME COVERED WITH BATTING AND FINAL MATERIAL

Fig. 8.18 Section view showing the construction of an upholstered piece of furniture.

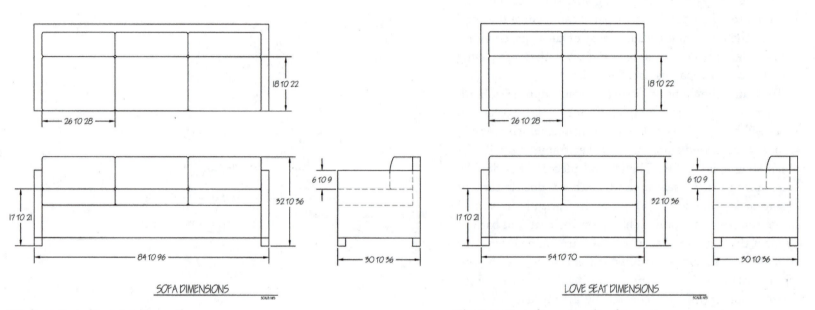

18 TO 22

26 TO 28

17 TO 21

32 TO 36

6 TO 9

84 TO 96

30 TO 36

SOFA DIMENSIONS
SCALE: NTS

18 TO 22

26 TO 28

17 TO 21

32 TO 36

6 TO 9

54 TO 70

30 TO 36

LOVE SEAT DIMENSIONS
SCALE: NTS

Fig. 8.19 Basic dimensions for a sofa.

Fig. 8.20 Basic dimensions for a love seat.

196

Lounge Chair

A lounge chair can be designed in a number of different ways, depending on the function and style of the space. The chair can be completely upholstered or have wood details; it can have arms or be an armless style; it can be a recliner or be designed with an ottoman. The seat height should be 17 to 21 inches from the floor, the depth of the seat should be 18 to 22 inches, and the width should be 20 to 24 inches for a small chair and 26 to 28 inches for a large chair. (See Figure 8.21.)

Just like the sofa, the quality and cost of a lounge chair is in its construction and materials. The subframe on a completely upholstered chair should be made from a hardwood such as ash, birch, maple, oak, or poplar. A lower-end chair will have a pine or some type of softwood frame. The designer should know what type of wood the custom builder is going to use. Depending on the style, the frame can be exposed, such as in an Art Deco design, which uses the contrast between the frame and cushion material as part of the design element. (See Figure 8.22.) Designs that use exposed frames must take into consideration the type of wood selected and the desired finish.

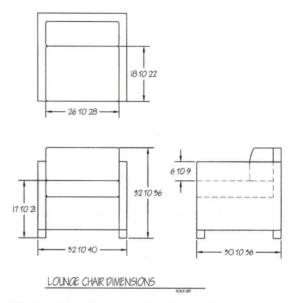

LOUNGE CHAIR DIMENSIONS
SCALE: NTS

Fig. 8.21 Basic dimensions for a lounge chair.

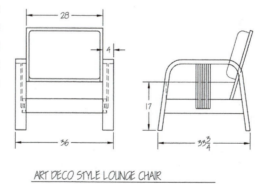

ART DECO STYLE LOUNGE CHAIR

Fig. 8.22 Example of an Art Deco lounge chair with exposed wood frame.

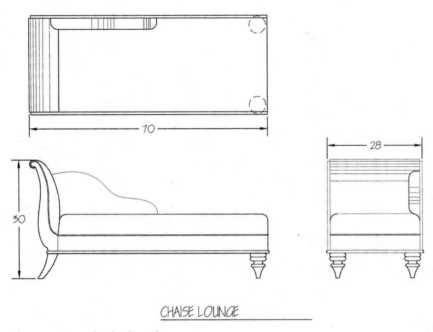

CHAISE LOUNGE

Fig. 8.23 Example of a chaise lounge.

Chaise Lounge

The French refer to this type of chair as a *chaise longue,* which means "long chair," but it is commonly known as a chaise lounge in English. A chaise lounge is like a stretched lounge chair. This type of chair was originally created in Egypt, although its name comes from France. This type of furniture became popular during the Rococo era in France because of its asymmetrical design. A chaise lounge can be designed as a completely upholstered piece or with an exposed wood frame structure with an upholstered seat, back, and possibly one or two sides or arms. The dimensions can vary, but the seat height should range from 15 inches to 20 inches. The depth can be from 24 inches to 32 inches, and the total overall length can be from 70 inches to 80 inches. This piece of furniture is usually designed as a reading area and is a freestanding single piece, but many sectional sofas have an optional chaise incorporated into the complete sectional design. (See Figure 8.23.)

Ottoman

An ottoman is an upholstered footrest that typically matches the style of a particular lounge chair or sofa. The total height can range from 15 inches to 20 inches, depending on the style and the height of the lounge chair or sofa seat. Ottomans are usually square or rectangular, depending on the width of the furniture they are going to be placed in front of. In smaller spaces, the ottoman can be designed for storage by hinging the top cushion so that the interior space is accessible. (See Figure 8.24.) Also, just like the lounge chair, the ottoman can be fully upholstered or have an exposed wood frame. In some designs, the exposed wood frame holds the cushion in place or has a reversible cushion with a hard surface at the bottom so that the ottoman can function as a small table when the cushion is flipped.

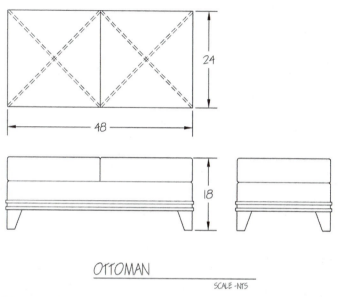

OTTOMAN
SCALE -NTS

Fig. 8.24 Example of an ottoman.

Chapter 8 Project and Quiz

Project 1

LIVING ROOM SET

Directions: Create visual drawings and details of a living room set so that you will be able to design related furniture pieces for a grouping. Choose a furniture style and repeat the details and elements for each of the pieces below:

1. End table
2. Coffee table
3. Sofa table

Part 1: Create a thumbnail sketch for each piece in your grouping.
Part 2: Create an orthographic projected drawing for each piece.
Part 3: Create a color rendering of one of the pieces.

Project 2

LARGE FURNITURE PROBLEMS

Directions: Create visual drawings and details of large pieces of furniture so that you will be able to design furniture without weight and scale problems. Design two different entertainment armoires. The first piece should be a corner cabinet armoire that has a historical influence, and the second should be a contemporary three-piece wall unit design using veneers to create visual interest. Each design must have space for a TV, a DVD player, a DVR, and a cable box.

Part 1: Show the armoires in elevation and side views. Label and show dimensions.

Part 2: Show the armoires with doors open and label the interior details with dimensions.

Part 3: Create one color rendering of an elevation view for each armoire.

Quiz

1. What is the correct height for a coffee table?
    A. 12" to 18"   B. 18" to 20"   C. 20" to 24"

2. When fitting stone or glass for a top surface to a wood frame, what should be the gap's dimension?
    A. ¹⁄₁₆" on all sides
    B. ⅛" on all sides
    C. ¼" on all sides

3. What is the basic height for an end table?
    A. 12"   B. 24"   C. 36"

4. What is the typical measurement of the side of an armoire?
    A. about 20"   B. about 24"   C. about 32"

5. What is meant by creating a double-wall armoire?
   A. doubling up the back
   B. doubling up the floor
   C. doubling up the sides

6. What do bifold doors have the ability to do?
   A. fold around the outside
   B. fold in the center when open
   C. open and slide

7. What is a typical seat-height dimension for a sofa,
   love seat, or lounge chair?
   A. 10" to 12"   B. 17" to 21"   C. 20" to 24"

8. A high-quality sofa frame is constructed from what
   type of material?
   A. plywood   B. softwood   C. hardwood

9. What does the French term *chaise longue* mean?
   A. wide chair   B. short chair   C. long chair

10. What should the width typically be for a sofa table?
    A. 6" to 11"   B. 12" to 18"   C. 18" to 24"

CHAPTER 9

Home Office Furniture Design

THE HOME OFFICE is a growing market in the furniture and interior design industry. This chapter starts with desks, showing different options for storage and discussing how today's technology applies to the desk. The goal is to provide an understanding of the need to balance design and function. Basic desk and drawer dimensions are provided as well as relating chair dimensions to the desk, as they go hand in hand. This chapter also covers the hotel desk to illustrate the differences between it and a home desk. Storage needs in the home office are discussed, including the file cabinet and file and bookcase dimensions.

The Desk

Over the past 100 years, desk designs have changed drastically, largely because the purpose of the desk has changed from a simple writing surface to a computer area. The computer should be designed into the desk from the beginning so that the desk will be as functional as possible. For example, the pencil drawer has been replaced with the keyboard tray, and some side drawers have been replaced with the CPU holder. You will need to configure the wiring, venting, and accessories such as the printer, scanner, and monitor. The most important dimension for any desk, however, is the work surface height. It should be the same height as a dining table, 29 to 30 inches tall. This is based on the ergonomics of a seated person.

Older desk designs, such as the secretary desk and the rolltop desk, still are good writing desks, but typically these desks do not work well with a computer because they have a closed top to conceal the work space, and this work space is too small in both height and overall depth to accommodate a desktop computer. However, some companies are reproducing these types of desks to look like an original piece, but they are designed to hold a computer and other electronic items.

Kneehole Desk

The kneehole desk is designed with a set of drawers on each side and a pencil drawer in the center that creates a space for the user's knees under the desk. The drawer sets on each side typically have two storage drawers above one large file drawer. There is also a full- or partial-depth modesty panel between these sides on the back of the desk.

Secretary Desk

A secretary desk looks like a small dresser with a folding front panel that, when open, makes up the writing surface. (See Figure 9.1a.) This panel can be vertical or slanted at an angle when closed. The inside has storage space for paperwork and possibly some small drawers or slotted storage areas. (See Figure 9.1b.) When the top is open, it is supported by a bottom drawer or support piece on each side.

Rolltop Desk

A rolltop desk has the same type of storage as a secretary desk but is larger in size. It gets its name from the top front rolling tambour-style door. The top of the piece features a beaded front that rolls up into the back of the

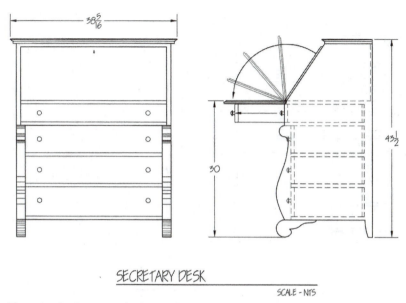

SECRETARY DESK

SCALE - NTS

Fig. 9.1a An Empire-style slant-top secretary desk. This design uses the first drawer to support the weight of the top when open.

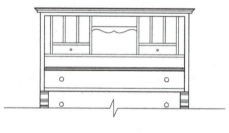

SECRETARY DESK (open interior view)

SCALE - NTS

Fig. 9.1b Interior view showing typical storage for paper and mail.

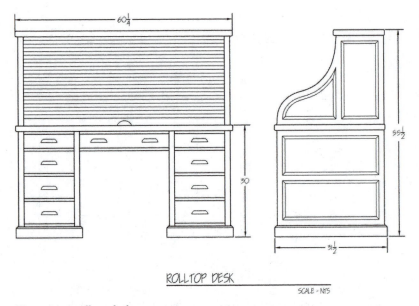

ROLLTOP DESK
SCALE - NTS

Fig. 9.2a A rolltop desk.

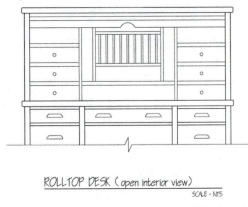

ROLLTOP DESK (open interior view)
SCALE - NTS

Fig. 9.2b Interior view showing typical storage for paper.

desk so that it is out of sight. The bottom of the desk is designed like a kneehole desk. (See Figures 9.2a and 9.2b.)

Modular-Style Desk

The modular-style desk uses modular components with a desktop. This style was created to take advantage of mass-production techniques so that a manufacturing company can produce many different versions of the same piece with the same parts. Then clients can pick and choose the pieces to create their design. These components can consist of a file drawer, stack of drawers, CPU holder, or storage bin, for example. (See Figures 9.3a through d.)

Creating a Dramatic Look with a Simple Design

When a piece like a desk has simple design elements, the objective is to make it interesting by using an appropriate level of detail to arrive at a design solution that satisfies the client's needs and budget. One way to accomplish this is to make sure that the elements work well with one another. The piece featured in Figure 9.4a through f uses a couple of different elements. The first is that the surface planes intersect each other with contrasting wood tones for emphasis. When creating a feature like this, it is important to make sure that each piece intersects in a way that allows the piece to remain functional. The top was

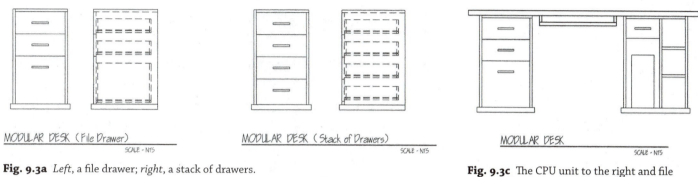

MODULAR DESK (File Drawer)
SCALE - NTS

MODULAR DESK (Stack of Drawers)
SCALE - NTS

MODULAR DESK
SCALE - NTS

Fig. 9.3a *Left*, a file drawer; *right*, a stack of drawers.

Fig. 9.3c The CPU unit to the right and file drawer unit to the left with a desktop and keyboard drawer.

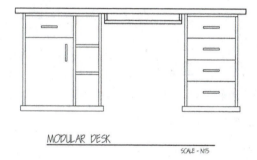

MODULAR DESK (CPU Holder)
SCALE - NTS

MODULAR DESK (Storage)
SCALE - NTS

MODULAR DESK
SCALE - NTS

Fig. 9.3b *Left*, a CPU holder and shelves; *right*, a drawer and door with shelves.

Fig. 9.3d A drawer unit to the right and file drawer and door unit to the left with a desktop and keyboard drawer.

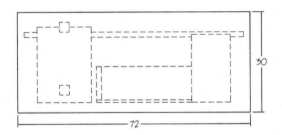

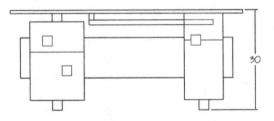

OFFICE COMPUTER DESK

SCALE: 1"=1'-0"

Fig. 9.4a AutoCAD images of an office computer desk.

Fig. 9.4b Photo of desk from front.

Fig. 9.4c Photo of desk from back.

Fig. 9.4d Detail of drawer and CPU door closed.

Fig. 9.4e Detail of drawer open and CPU door closed.

Fig. 9.4f Detail of drawer closed and CPU door open.

208

designed to have a floating quality, which helps the overall visual weight of the piece. Note that the details on the drawers and CPU door repeat the intersecting planes and contrasting tones. Because the piece has such a simple layout, the drawer pulls should match the overall style. In this piece, instead of using store-bought pulls, the handles are negative-space square openings that match the rectilinear design. They are also asymmetrical to match the asymmetrical design of the overall desk.

Hotel-Style Desk

For many people today, the hotel room is their home away from home, and the hotel desk functions as their office. A hotel-style desk is similar to a home office desk but is designed to fit the aesthetics of the hotel room. The two major differences are that the unit does not feature file drawers because storage is not a priority, and the unit has electrical and Internet outlets built into the desk so that a business traveler can use a laptop computer. The desk shown in Figure 9.5 addresses two different problems: creating various types of curved wood surfaces and the handling of both Internet and power connections to the desk. The example shown is a contemporary desk, and because the finish surface will be a veneer, the substrate can be MDF. MDF creates a good flat surface; however, if the budget is not sufficient to specify MDF, then particleboard may be used.

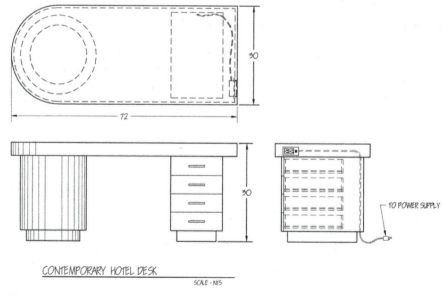

Fig. 9.5 Example of a contemporary desk for a hotel room application.

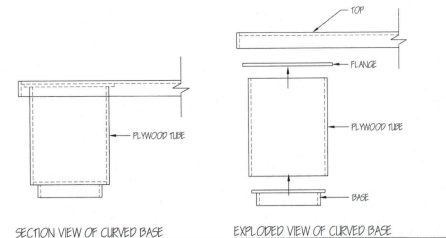

SECTION VIEW OF CURVED BASE

EXPLODED VIEW OF CURVED BASE

Fig. 9.6a Section view of the tube base of the desk.

Fig. 9.6b Exploded view showing base and top flange, which are glued to the plywood tube creating the complete base. Then the base is screwed to the top through the flange.

If the desktop has a curve, bender board can be used to form the outside edge. This outside edge is doubled up because bender board is only ⅜ inch thick; doubling creates a ¾-inch outside edge that is glued to the MDF top surface. Veneer is then glued to these surfaces, creating a wood appearance. With this design, the right side has a stack of drawers that creates the same foot detail and finish as the tube pedestal on the left. (See Figure 9.6a.) This drawing shows a tube pedestal design on one side of the desk, which is created by using a pre-bought plywood tube. Many companies make plywood tubes in standard dimensions from 3 inches to 48 inches diameter. They are available in whole and half tubes and are typically 12 to 48 inches long. They are ⅜ inch thick with a veneer finish around the outside. The tube is ordered by diameter, length, and wood finish. Once the tube is chosen, a flange is created at the top of the tube using ¾-inch plywood so that it can be attached to the top itself. A foot detail or molding is added to protect the bottom plywood edge of the tube. (See Figure 9.6b.)

The desk also needs to accommodate the use of laptop computers and an Internet connection in the hotel room. The electrical and Internet connections can be added and are available in many different configurations. Because this desk is for hotel use, the type of terminal that should be used is designed to mount to the front or side of the desk. This protects it from anything being spilled on the desk. The terminal is installed into the desk, and

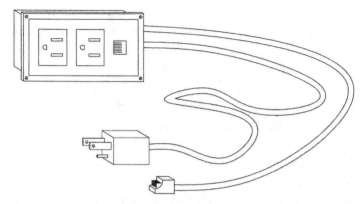

Fig. 9.7a Example of power and Internet terminals for furniture applications.

Fig. 9.7b Example of an installed unit from the front.

Fig. 9.7c Example of an installed unit from the inside.

the cords are contained within the desk and run out the back, plugging into the power and Internet supply. (See Figures 9.7a through c.)

Office Chair

The office chair can be designed to match the style of the desk and generally incorporates a swivel base. Stationary office chairs that do not have adjustment features are also available but are seldom used today. The swivel base is available in a number of different styles and sizes; choices

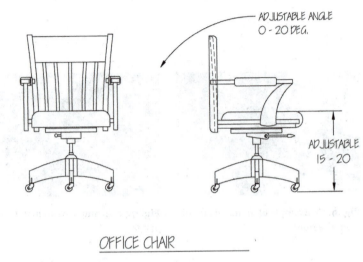

ADJUSTABLE ANGLE
0 - 20 DEG.

ADJUSTABLE
15 - 20

OFFICE CHAIR

Fig. 9.8 Example of an office chair.

depend on the type of chair. Bases are adjustable so that the seat height can be raised or lowered to fit the needs of the end user. An office chair seat should be adjustable between 15 and 20 inches. (See Figure 9.8.) The base is made of steel or high-impact plastic, but the legs can be skinned over in wood to match other parts of the chair. The base has casters, so it can roll and swivel from side to side as well as having the ability to lean back. The angle of most desk chairs can be adjusted, and the typical range is between 0 and 20 degrees. The designer should provide the appropriate type of base to the fabricator so that the final chair will be identical to what was designed. The seat and back of the chair will be constructed by the fabricator, finished, and upholstered before being mounted to the base. The bottom of the seat is mounted with screws to a flange on the steel base; typically a total of six to eight screws connect the two.

File Cabinet

There are two basic types of file storage: the file cabinet that arranges the file drawers vertically, making for a tall piece of furniture, and a credenza that arranges the drawers horizontally, creating a low, wide piece of furniture. The file cabinet or credenza needs to be designed around the dimensions of the files it will contain and how they will be stored within the credenza, either vertically or horizontally. File drawer hardware is slightly different from a standard drawer slide. It still mounts on the side of the drawer but is designed to handle more weight. The basic dimensions of a hanging file are 9¼ inches tall and 11¾ inches wide with a ½-inch hanger on each side, creating a total width of 12¾ inches. However, a legal file measures 9¼ inches by 14¾ inches. (See Figure 9.9a.)

On the inside of the file drawer, a metal band is added to each side for the hanging files to rest on. This is done by adding metal to the side, so that it stands over the side wall by ½ inch, or by making it fit to the inside of the side wall by hanging on an extra piece of wood that is mounted to the side wall. The overall dimensions differ between these two styles, which are shown in Figure 9.9b.

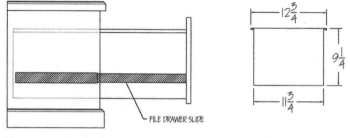

Fig. 9.9a *Left*, the drawer slide mount from the side; *right*, the basic dimension of a standard hanging file.

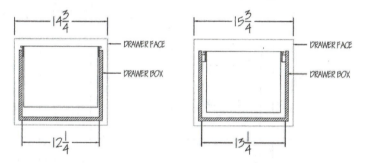

Fig. 9.9b *Left*, a hanging file hanging above the drawer box; *right*, a hanging file hanging inside the draw box.

Bookcase

A bookcase generally is narrow, about 12 inches deep, in order to display books for easy access. The shelves are made from ¾-inch plywood with some type of solid wood front edge. This edge can be ¾ inch by ¾ inch or ¾ inch by 1½ inches, depending on the desired aesthetic. (See Figure

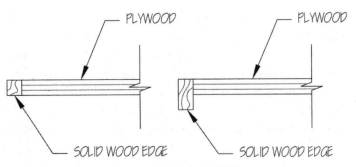

Fig. 9.10 Section detail of two different shelf edges.

9.10.) If the front edge is 1½ inches, it will strengthen the shelf a little, but the main reason for having a wider edge is to create a better proportion between the shelf and the rest of the piece.

The overall span of a bookshelf should be a maximum length of 36 inches. If the bookshelf is designed to hold heavier items such as law books, then the total span should be a maximum length of 32 inches. This will ensure that the shelf will not start to bow from the weight over time. (See Figure 9.11.)

Bookcase/Curio Cabinet

One way to increase the length of a shelf is to add a center support; if doors are added then that support can become part of the design. This center piece can have the same holes drilled that are on the sides of the piece for

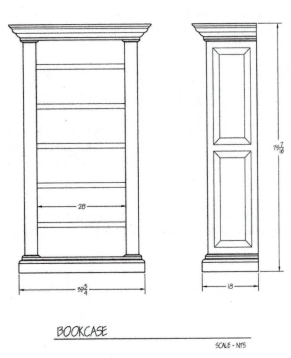

BOOKCASE

SCALE - NTS

Fig. 9.11 A bookcase with architectural details. This piece has double-wall construction, so that the total shelf length is 28″.

the shelf support pegs. The shelf pegs allow the shelving to be adjustable so that the piece can conform to the books or items that are displayed. To still give the look of a bookcase, the doors can be a wood frame with a glass panel. (See Figures 9.12a and 9.12b.) The glass panel can be attached to the frame in many ways. The best way to create a clean finished look to the inside of the door is to attach a wood support to the back edge to hold the glass in place.

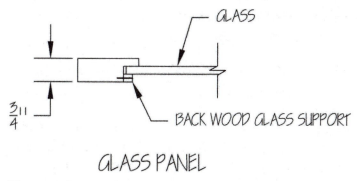

GLASS PANEL

Fig. 9.12a Section view of how a glass panel door is constructed.

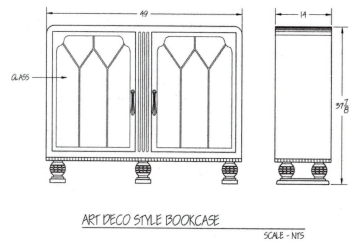

ART DECO STYLE BOOKCASE

SCALE - NTS

Fig. 9.12b An Art Deco bookcase; total interior shelf length is 47½" with a center shelf support.

APPLIED MOLDING
TO DRAWER FACE

RAISED PANEL

MODESTY PANEL

HOME OFFICE DESK

SCALE 1" = 1'-0"

Fig. 9.13a Example in AutoCAD (orthographic projection) of a desk made from solid wood, with pieces labeled and showing dimensions.

Chapter 9 Project and Quiz

Project 1

DESK DESIGN

Directions: Create gesture drawings of different desk designs to show a basic understanding of proportions and human ergonomics as they relate to furniture design. Draw two different desk designs, one constructed from solid wood that has a historical influence and one constructed with veneers to create a contemporary modern look.

Part 1: Concept sketch: Create pencil and/or technical pen drawings. Draw each in orthographic and perspective views.

Part 2: AutoCAD: Create both pieces of furniture in Auto-CAD (orthographic projection), as shown in Chapter 2. Label the pieces and show dimensions. Print them out at ¾-inch or 1-inch scale. (See the examples in Figures 9.13a and 9.13b.)

Part 3: Color renderings: On an 8½-by-11 sheet of paper, marker-render one drawing of each idea.

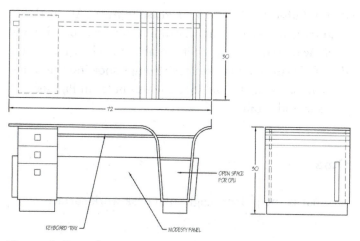

Fig. 9.13b Example in AutoCAD (orthographic projection) of a desk made from veneers, with pieces labeled and showing dimensions.

Project 2

BOOKCASE DESIGN

Directions: Create two sets of drawing for the same design —one orthographic drawing showing the complete piece with dimensions and labeling and one section drawing showing the construction of the piece.

Part 1: Concept sketch: Create pencil and/or technical pen drawings. Create thumbnail sketches from front and side views while changing details, proportions, and elements in order to develop each idea.

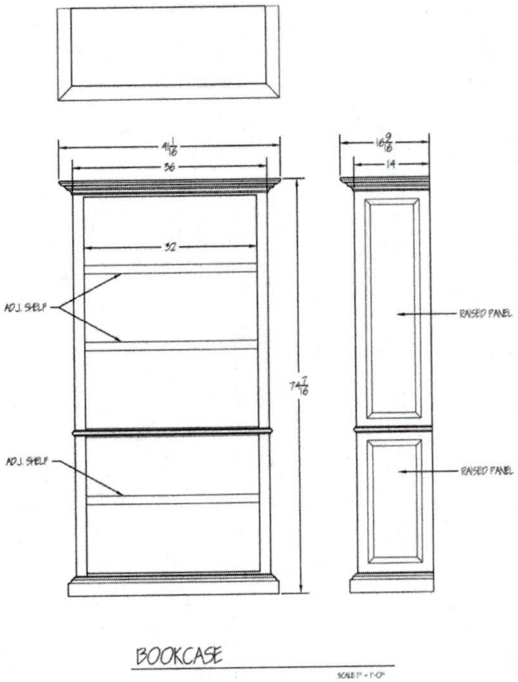

BOOKCASE

Fig. 9.14a Example of an orthographic projection of bookcase in AutoCAD, with labels and dimensions.

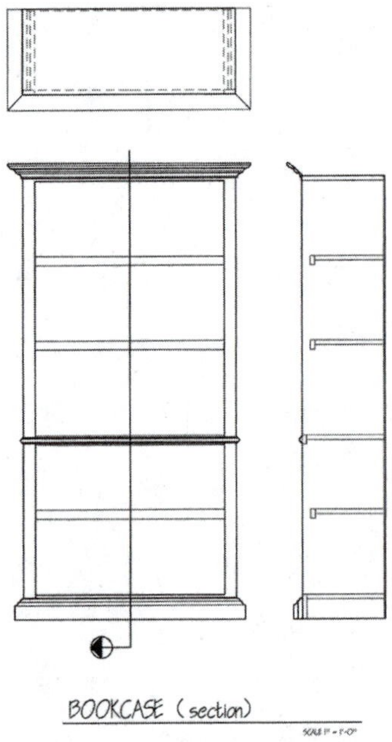

BOOKCASE (section)

Fig. 9.14b Example of a second set of drawings showing the same bookcase in Figure 9.14a as a section.

Part 2: AutoCAD: Create a bookcase in AutoCAD (orthographic projection), as shown in Chapter 2. Label it and show dimensions. Print it out at ¾-inch or 1-inch scale.

Part 3: Create a second set of drawings showing the same bookcase as a section. (See the examples in Figures 9.14a and 9.14b.)

Quiz

1. What is the proper height of a desk work surface?
    A. 30"   B. 32"   C. 36"

2. How is a secretary desk designed?
    A. the face rolls up
    B. the front folds down
    C. the front slides out

3. What is the maximum span of a shelf in a bookcase?
    A. 24"   B. 36"   C. 48"

4. What is meant by a modular design?
    A. using the same components over and over again
    B. creating a modern look to the piece
    C. creating a one-of-a-kind piece

5. What type of drawer slide should a filing cabinet use?
    A. a standard slide
    B. a doubled-up standard slide
    C. a specific file slide

6. What is the typical wall thickness of a plywood manufactured tube?
   A. ⅜"   B. ½"   C. ¾"

7. What is the typical adjustable height for an office
   chair seat?
   A. 10" to 15"   B. 12" to 18"   C. 15" to 20"

8. What is the typical range that an office chair can be
   angled?
   A. 0 to 10 degrees
   B. 0 to 20 degrees
   C. 0 to 30 degrees

9. What is the best way to attach a glass panel to a
   door?
   A. glue the glass to the back edge of the door
   B. attach a wood support to the back edge of the
      door
   C. add screws to the back edge of the door

10. What type of desk has a beaded front door?
    A. secretary desk
    B. rolltop desk
    C. kneehole desk

CHAPTER 10

Designing Other Pieces of Furniture

THIS CHAPTER ILLUSTRATES some pieces of furniture that were not covered in previous chapters, including different types of drop leaf tables and game tables. These pieces can work in multiple types of rooms. Discussion also includes accessory pieces such as picture and mirror frames, as well as floating shelves. The chapter also discusses lamp construction, to show how the basic components fit into the design, and ready-to-assemble (RTA) furniture.

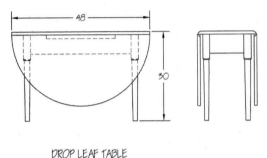

DROP LEAF TABLE

SCALE - NTS

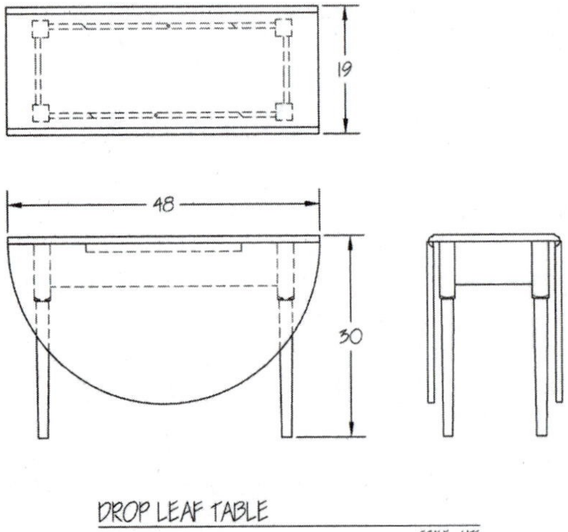

Fig. 10.1a Example of a drop leaf table with the leafs closed.

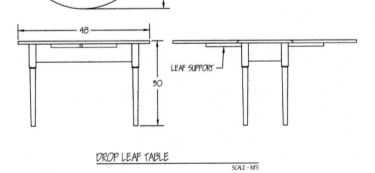

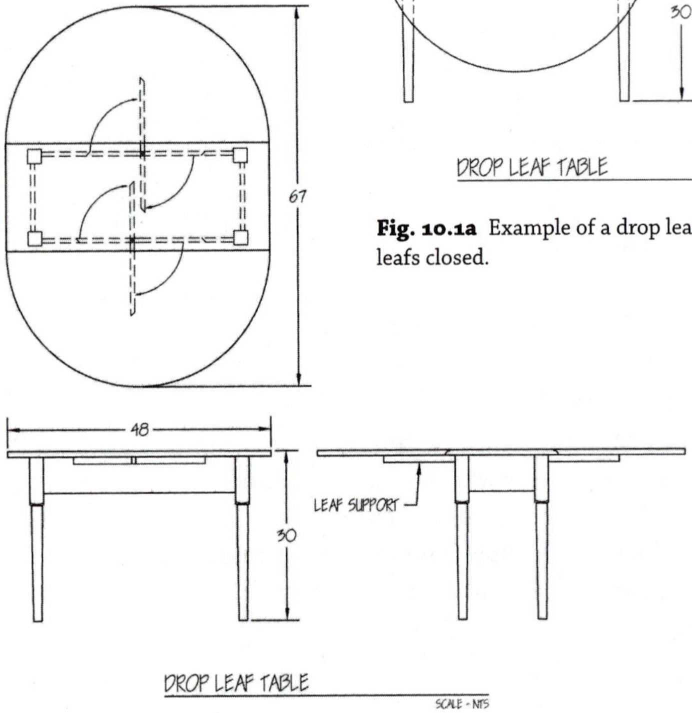

DROP LEAF TABLE

SCALE - NTS

Fig. 10.1b Example of a drop leaf table with the leafs raised.

Drop Leaf Table

A drop leaf table has two top sections that fold down from a center fixed top, creating a smaller overall table surface. The table can be used as a console table when the two leaves are down and as a dining table when raised. The table typically has a wooden arm that swings or slides from the underside of the base outward to support the raised top. (See Figures 10.1a and 10.1b.) Newer tables may have a metal bar that performs the same function. The profile of where the fixed top and leaf top come together is a radius bead on the fixed top and a radius cove on the leaf top with a special hinge on the underside of the tops. (See Figures 10.2a and 10.2b.) This allows the tops to create a tight fit when open.

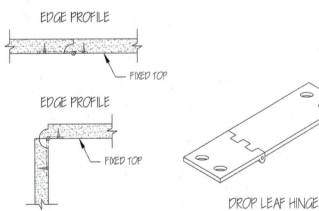

Fig. 10.2a Example of a drop leaf edge detail.

Fig. 10.2b Example of a drop leaf hinge.

Gateleg Table

A gateleg table is a type of drop leaf table with an extra leg and rail system on each side that opens like a fence gate, thus providing its name. When the leaves are dropped, the gateleg swings toward the frame, which removes the support to the leaf top. When both leaves are dropped, the table has a total of six legs under the fixed top, four that make up the table base and two gatelegs. The profile of the top is the same as a standard drop leaf table. (See Figures 10.3a and 10.3b.)

Restaurant-Style Drop Leaf Table

This type of table has a square fixed top with curved leaves on each side so that the table can change from a square four-person table to a round six-person table. (See Figures 10.4a and 10.4b.) This is done in a completely different way than a standard drop leaf table. The edge detail is at a square right angle to the top surface, with a piano hinge and a sliding locking or strong magnetic catch component underneath. The leaf locks to the underside of the table when it is not in use. When the table is expanded, the leaf is pulled down out of the lock position and swings 180 degrees to become level with the fixed top surface. The metal sliding lock is pulled outward to support the leaf from the underside. (See Figure 10.5.)

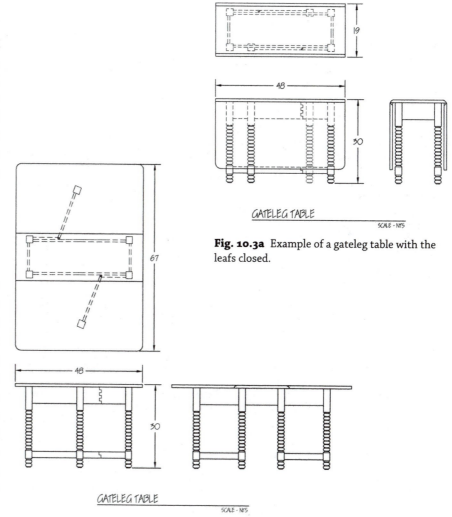

GATELEG TABLE
SCALE - NTS

Fig. 10.3a Example of a gateleg table with the leafs closed.

GATELEG TABLE
SCALE - NTS

Fig. 10.3b Example of a gateleg table with the leafs raised.

The bases for these tables are created from a prefabricated kit that is available through a variety of furniture-part companies. (See Figures 10.6a and 10.6b.) They can be found in many different styles and sizes as well as finishes. The width of the base depends on the size of the top; most companies state the recommended top size for the style of base available. Table 10.1 shows the appropriate base sizes for different top sizes, but each manufacturer specifies its own size dimensions.

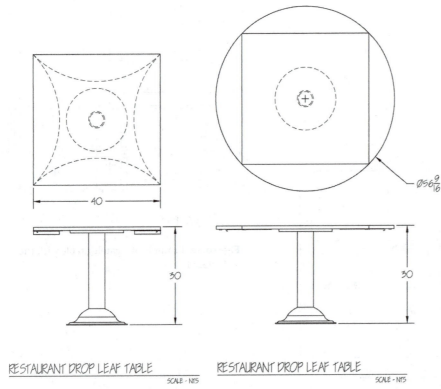

RESTAURANT DROP LEAF TABLE
SCALE - NTS

Fig. 10.4a Example of a restaurant-style drop leaf table with leafs closed.

RESTAURANT DROP LEAF TABLE
SCALE - NTS

Fig. 10.4b Example of a restaurant-style drop leaf table with leafs raised.

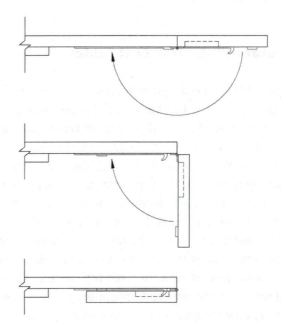

Fig. 10.5 Example of how the leaf system works.

Table 10.1

Base versus Top Sizes: X-Style and Table Disk-Style Bases

X-Style Base	Square Top Size	Round Top Size
22″ × 22″ spread	24″ to 30″	30″ to 36″
30″ × 30″ spread	36″	42″
36″ × 36″ spread	42″ to 48″	48″
	Rectangle Top Size	
24″ × 30″ spread	30″ × 36″ to 36″ × 48″	

Table Disk-Style Base	Square Top Size	Round Top Size
18″ diameter	24″	24″ to 30″
24″ diameter	36″	36″ to 42″
30″ diameter	42″	42″ to 48″

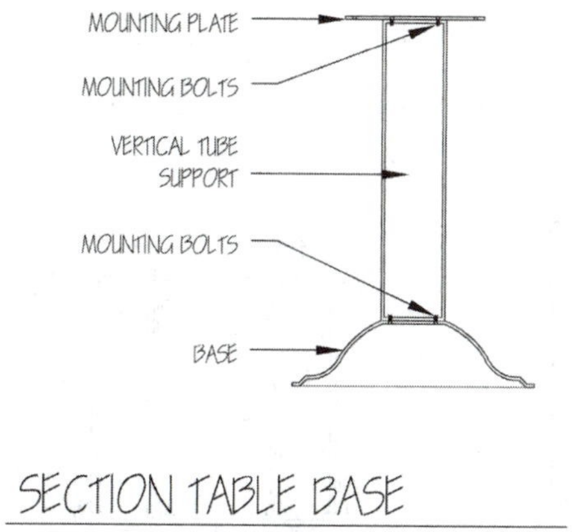

SECTION TABLE BASE

Fig. 10.6a Example of a prefabricated table base kit as a section view.

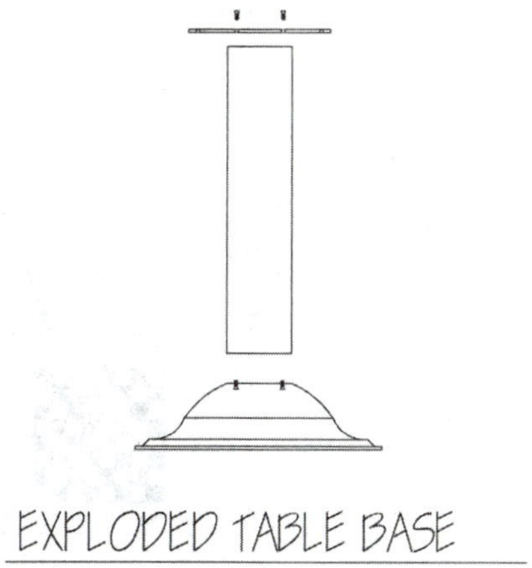

EXPLODED TABLE BASE

Fig. 10.6b Example of a prefabricated table base kit in an exploded view.

Game Table

A game table can be designed in a number of ways; the material for the top surface can also vary depending on the type of game being played. To make a universal game table the game-board top should be reversible. This can be done by making the complete top fit into pegs in the base so that it can be taken off and flipped from a felt surface for playing cards to a wood surface for board games. Two other ways are to have a center piece of the top that can be flipped from a leather surface to a wood surface or to

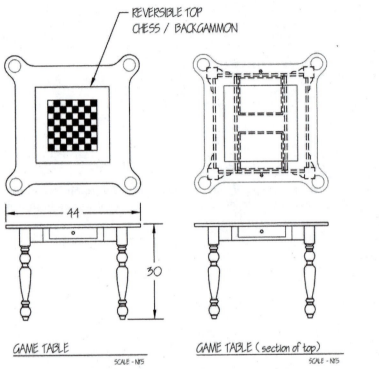

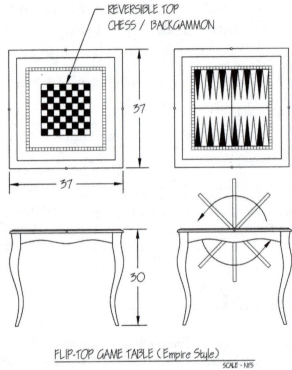

Fig. 10.7 *Left*, example of a game table with a reversible game top; *right*, section view of a table with drawers.

Fig. 10.8 Example of a flip-top game table. The image on the right shows how the top is flipped.

have the board be part of the tabletop, such as a chess-board top that can be flipped to a backgammon-board top. (See Figure 10.7.)

The construction of a game table is basically the same as for a small dining table. The base has legs that are connected to aprons by mortise-and-tenon joints or biscuit joints, and the top is held in place with pocket screws. The center flippable game board should be flush with the top.

Flip-Top Game Table

This is a simple type of table where the top is hinged in the center to an outside frame. The hinge is a metal rod that fits into a hole in the side of the game board and the side of the table frame. The center pivots on the metal rod on each side so that the top can spin from one side to the other. Once the top is flipped, a pin locks the top in place from the opposite side of the pivot. (See Figure 10.8.)

Fold-Out Table

This type of table has a foldable top that can spin and open to increase the overall size of the tabletop. When the top is closed, the piece can be used as a console table, which takes up less space. Then it can be folded open to become a small dining table or game table. (See Figures 10.9a and 10.9b.)

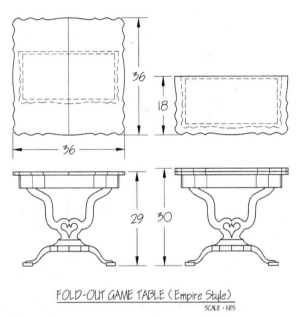

FOLD-OUT GAME TABLE (Empire Style)
SCALE - NTS

Fig. 10.9a A fold-out table; the top will double in size.

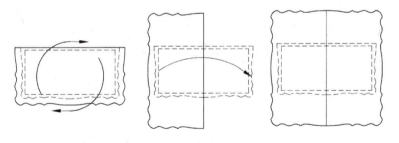

FOLD-OUT GAME TABLE (Top Detail)

Fig. 10.9b How the top spins and then folds open.

The top is hinged so that when it is closed the top is stacked on top of itself. The top spins to a right angle of its original position and then opens, which doubles the size of the top. Therefore, a closed 18-inch-by-36-inch table can open to create a 36-inch-by-36-inch tabletop.

Hall Chair

A hall chair can serve many different functions depending on how it is designed. This piece is placed by the front door or in the front hall of the home and is used for storage, as a coat rack, and as a seat for getting ready to go out or for removing boots. Hall chairs are typically tall so that a mirror can be added to the back of the chair. Metal coat hooks are added to the top of the back stiles of the chair, and the top of the seat is hinged for storage inside the box-style seat. (See Figure 10.10.)

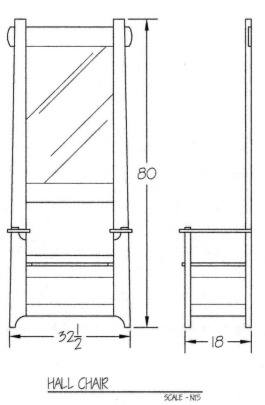

HALL CHAIR

SCALE - NTS

Fig. 10.10 Example of an Arts and Crafts–style hall chair with mirror.

Bench

A bench has the same dimensions as a chair; the seat height should be 15 to 20 inches from the floor, and the piece can have a back or just be a surface plane for a seat. The bench can be designed for a single person or more, typically two to four persons. The room or hall size dictates the overall dimensions. If the piece is an outdoor bench, then the best wood to use is teak. Teak has natural oils in the wood that protect it from the elements. (See Figures 10.11a through c.)

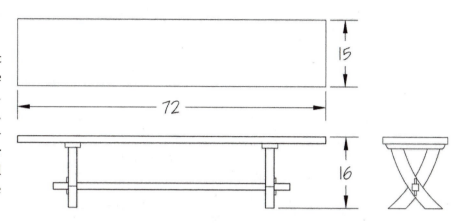

ARTS AND CRAFTS STYLE BENCH

SCALE - NTS

Fig. 10.11b Example of an Arts and Crafts style bench.

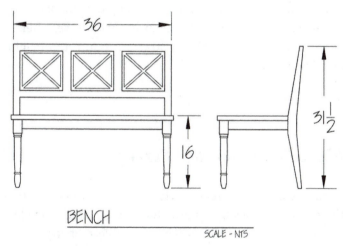

BENCH

SCALE - NTS

Fig. 10.11a Example of a small two-person bench with a back.

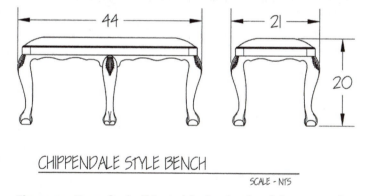

CHIPPENDALE STYLE BENCH

SCALE - NTS

Fig. 10.11c Example of a Chippendale claw-foot bench for two people.

Barstool

Barstools are constructed in the same way as dining chairs. There are two main differences, however. The first is the seat height and total height, which is much higher than a typical chair. The second is that stretchers need to be added to the legs of the piece for strength and for the users to be able to rest their feet on.

Typically, there are two main sizes for barstools; the size to use is based on the height of the countertop. A countertop that is a standard 36-inch kitchen height uses a barstool with a seat height of 26 inches, which is known as a low barstool. If the countertop height is 40 inches tall, then a barstool with a 30-inch seat height, or tall barstool, is needed. A basic rule of thumb is that the seat height of the barstool is 10 inches below the countertop height. (See Figure 10.12.)

Fig. 10.12 *Left,* a low barstool—seat height 26″; *right,* a tall barstool —seat height 30″.

Picture Frame or Mirror

A picture frame is created with mitered corners so that the end grain does not show. One way to attach the glass and image or mirror is to have a double rabbet joint on the inside back edge of the frame material. The first rabbet holds the glass and the image or mirror while the second holds the backing material, which is typically ¼-inch plywood. That material is then screwed to the back of the frame. When adding the hanging wire, the mounts should be attached to the back sides of the frame. This allows the weight to be distributed evenly. (See Figures 10.13.a and 10.13b.)

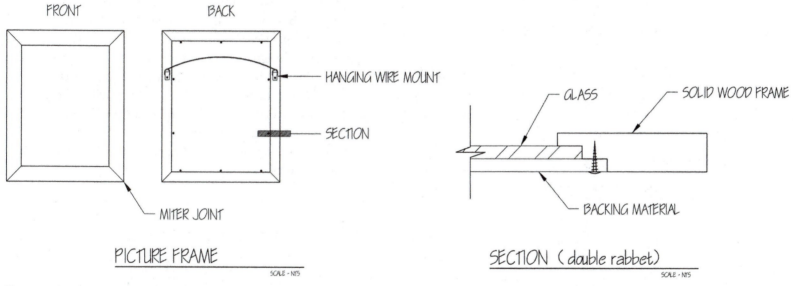

Fig. 10.13a *Left,* a miter joint from the front; *right,* the hanging wire on the back.

Fig. 10.13b Section view of a double rabbet joint showing frame, glass, and backing.

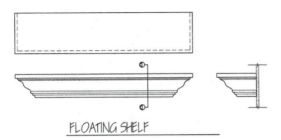

Fig. 10.14a Orthographic view of a floating shelf.

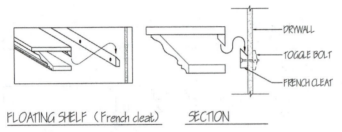

Fig. 10.14b Detail of a French-cleat-mount floating shelf.

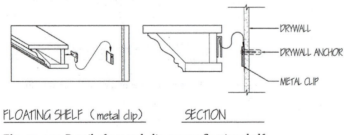

Fig. 10.14c Detail of a metal-clip-mount floating shelf.

Floating Shelf

A floating shelf can be designed, constructed, and installed in many different ways. The drawing in Figure 10.14a shows a shelf with a crown molding detail; the detail is both decorative and functional because it creates a hollow interior space for the mounting hardware. The shelf can be mounted to the wall using a French cleat, a pair of metal support clips, or special screw pins, depending on how it is designed. (See Figures 10.14b through d.) Each style of mounting hardware uses a two-part system where one part is attached to the back of the shelf and the other part is attached to the wall. Then the shelf is placed into the bracket on the wall, which supports the weight of the shelf. This allows the shelf to appear to be attached without any visible screws.

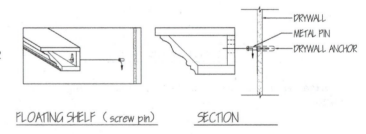

Fig. 10.14d Detail of a screw-pin-mount floating shelf.

Reception Desk

A reception desk is designed to the client's requirements. It is typically the first thing that someone will see when walking into a corporate office, and because it is a public space, the desk needs to be designed to be ADA (Americans with Disabilities Act) compliant. This means that part of the countertop height must be a maximum of 34 inches tall with a writing surface. (See Figure 10.15.) This can be accomplished by stepping down the front of the desk from a height of 42 inches to the 34-inch ADA transaction height.

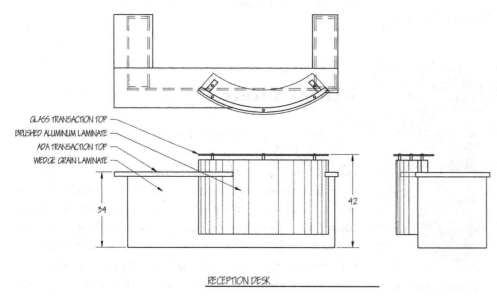

GLASS TRANSACTION TOP
BRUSHED ALUMINUM LAMINATE
ADA TRANSACTION TOP
WEDGE GRAIN LAMINATE

34

42

RECEPTION DESK

Fig. 10.15 Orthographic projection of a reception desk.

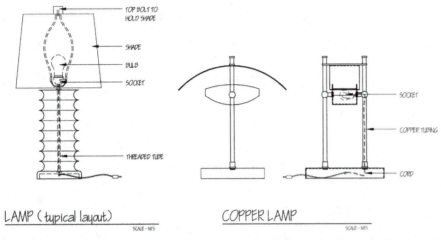

LAMP (typical layout)
SCALE - NTS

TOP BOLT TO HOLD SHADE
SHADE
BULB
SOCKET
THREADED TUBE

COPPER LAMP
SCALE - NTS

SOCKET
COPPER TUBING
CORD

Fig. 10.16a A table lamp with turned wood base and typical shade.

Fig. 10.16b A floor lamp made of metal with a curved metal shade.

Basic Lighting Fixture Configuration

A lighting fixture includes some basic components for the electrical parts: bulb, socket, threaded tube, cord, plugs, and washers and nuts. One main detail is to design the piece so that the cord is hidden inside the fixture. The threaded tube mounts the socket to the fixture and allows the cord to travel to the bottom. If the fixture has a wood base, a hole is drilled for the threaded tube. If the piece is metal, then metal tubing can be used to solve the same problem. (See Figures 10.16a through c.)

Fig. 10.16c A photograph of a copper lamp with a metal shade.

RTA Furniture

RTA, or ready-to-assemble, furniture—also known as KD, or knock-down, furniture—is made oversveas and is typically of lower quality because of the materials used, mostly particleboard covered with a laminate, and also because it is not a solid complete piece. Manufacturers create ready-to-assemble furniture to cut down on the shipping cost, because the piece takes up less space while disassembled; this also lowers the production cost. These types of pieces have their own special connections that allow the end user to assemble the piece with simple tools.

Chapter 10 Projects and Quiz

Project 1

DROP LEAF TABLE

Directions: Create one set of drawings for either a standard drop leaf table or a gateleg table. The set should include standard orthographic projection and any other details that are needed to illustrate the construction and character of the piece.

Part 1: Create a minimum of 10 thumbnail sketches to design the proportions and details of the piece.

Part 2: From the sketches create AutoCAD or manual drafted drawings as orthographic projections in ¾-inch or 1-inch scale. Include the following:

  A. orthographic of the overall design; label materials and show dimensions
  B. orthographic of the construction showing hidden lines
  C. details to show the character of the piece, such as edge profile

Part 3: Marker rendering: reprint one orthographic projection piece and render all views; create material surfaces, highlights, and shadows.

Project 2

GAME TABLE

Directions: Create one set of drawings for either a standard game table, a flip-top game table, or a fold-out game table. The set should include standard orthographic projection and any other details that are needed to show the construction and character of the piece.

Part 1: Create a minimum of 10 thumbnail sketches to design the proportions and details of the piece.

Part 2: From the sketches create AutoCAD or manual drafted drawings as orthographic projections in ¾-inch or 1-inch scale. Include the following:

  A. orthographic of the overall design; label materials and show dimensions
  B. orthographic of the construction showing hidden lines
  C. details showing the character of the piece

Part 3: Marker rendering: reprint one orthographic projection piece and render all views; create material surfaces, highlights, and shadows.

Project 3

BARSTOOLS

Directions: Create two sets of drawings, one each of a low and high barstool, showing construction with hidden lines and an understanding of ergonomics and how the stool relates to the countertop.

Part 1: Create a minimum of 10 thumbnail sketches to design the proportions and details of the pieces.

Part 2: From the sketches create AutoCAD or manual drafted drawings as orthographic projections in ¾-inch or 1-inch scale. Include the following for each barstool:

    A. orthographic of the overall design; label materials and show dimensions
    B. orthographic of the construction showing hidden lines
    C. details showing the character of the piece

Part 3: Marker rendering: reprint one orthographic projection piece and render all views; create material surfaces, highlights, and shadows.

Project 4

MIRROR

Directions: Create visual drawings of a mirror design, showing construction using hidden lines with details.

Part 1: Create a minimum of 10 thumbnail sketches to design the proportions and details of the piece.

Part 2: From the sketches create AutoCAD or manual drafted drawings as orthographic projections in ¾-inch or 1-inch scale. Include the following:

    A. orthographic of the overall design; label materials and show dimensions

    B. drawing of the back showing the hanging wire

    C. section detail showing frame, mirror, and backing material

Part 3: Marker rendering: reprint one orthographic projection piece and render all views; create material surfaces, highlights, and shadows

Quiz

Directions: Circle the best answer choice for each of the following questions.

1. What is the correct height for a typical game table?
   A. 29″ to 30″   B. 32″ to 33″   C. 33″ to 36″

2. What best describes the profile edge of a drop leaf table?
   A. both edges are beveled at 30 degrees
   B. one edge is a cove and one is a bead
   C. one edge is straight and one is beveled

3. How many legs does a gateleg table with two drop leaves have?
   A. 4   B. 5   C. 6

4. What type of hinge is typically used on a restaurant drop leaf table?
   A. piano hinge
   B. drop leaf hinge
   C. concealed hinge

5. What is the typical seat height for a bench?
   A. 10″ to 13″   B. 15″ to 20″   C. 20″ to 23″

6. What is the correct seat height for a tall barstool?
   A. 26″   B. 30″   C. 36″

7. What is the correct seat height for a low barstool?
   A. 26″   B. 30″   C. 36″

8. What is the maximum height for a reception desk
   countertop in order to be ADA compliant?
   A. 34″   B. 36″   C. 42″

9. Which of the following is not a typical lamp part?
   A. socket   B. shroud   C. bulb

10. What does RTA stand for?
    A. regular travel assembly
    B. round table assembly
    C. ready to assemble

Glossary

A

Adam (1760–1790) A style of furniture; the name comes from British architect and designer Robert Adam. The pieces from this era typically had rectilinear forms with inlaid decoration, applied classical motifs, and sometimes painted surfaces.

Additive space To construct by continually adding onto the piece.

Alder Hardwood from North America that is light brown to light tan in color. Used in furniture construction, carving, and turning because of its soft nature and workability.

Apron A rail typically used under the dining tabletop that connects the legs.

Armoire A large freestanding piece of furniture that was traditionally used to store clothing but that today is designed as an entertainment center.

Art Deco (1920–1940) A style of furniture that had a big impact on architecture, automobile design, clothing, and graphic design as well as furniture. It uses inlay with curves while creating different surface planes as well as creating a balance between positive and negative space.

Art Nouveau (1890–1910) A style of furniture that was a continued reaction against the Victorian era. This style originated in France and features flowing curves and detailed patterns.

Arts and Crafts (1880–1910) A style of furniture that was a rebellion against Victorian industrialism. This is handcrafted furniture that emphasizes construction, using the joinery as a major design element. This style is also known as Mission style. *See also* Mission.

Ash Hardwood from North America that is light in color with a wide grain pattern used in furniture construction; it is also used in baseball bat manufacturing.

Asymmetrical An object that is not a mirror image of itself.

B

Balance Our perception of visual weight as it appears in design.

Ball and claw foot A carved detail that resembles a talon grasping a ball; typically found at the base of a cabriole leg.

Banding Inlay that creates a color or grain contrast along the perimeter of a surface, such as a detail around a desktop.

Bas relief *Bas* is Latin for "low"; bas relief is a carving that has a slight depth into the wood or material.

Beam A post structure; for example, the leg detail to a table.

Bergère (Louis XIV and XV era) An armchair with an upholstered back, closed upholstered sides, and a seat cushion.

Biedermeier (1815–1848) A style of furniture that typically uses blond woods combined with architectural details; this German style of furniture has curved lines and contrasting features. The name is not from a designer but from two German words combined: *bieder,* meaning "common" or "plain," and *Meier,* which is a common surname in Germany.

Bifold door A type of door that is hinged in the center so that when the door is opened it will fold in the center in order to take up less space when open.

Birch Hardwood from North America that is light in color with a straight to wide grain pattern. This wood has a similar color and grain pattern to maple.

Bombe A style of furniture in which the case bows outward on the sides and front; it typically contains drawers.

Bonnet top A design style with an arched top. One typical piece is the bonnet top armoire.

Book matching Wood is sliced in half to create a matching set. After being sliced. the pieces open like a book, which creates a mirrored symmetrical grain.

Boston rocker A chair that has the same style features as a Windsor chair but with turned spindles to create a rocker.

Brazilian cherry Hardwood from Latin America, also known as Jatoba, which is reddish-brown in color with a straight grain. This wood resembles North American cherry.

Breakfront A cabinet or hutch with a center section that has a deeper dimension than the two side pieces, which recess slightly.

Buffet Similar to a sideboard, this piece is used in the dining room and can have a top piece, making it a hutch or china cabinet.

Bunn foot A turned short leg typically used on upholstered furniture or case goods.

Burl A material that is made into a veneer and has a swirled design to the grain.

Butt joint A wood joint in which the pieces connect at a flat edge or are butted against one another.

C

Cabriole A bowed leg that has a tapered foot; typically found on Queen Anne–style furniture.

Camelback A design feature on sofas in which the back of the sofa has a center hump.

Cane A style of seat using rattan that is woven into patterns, creating a light feel to the seat.

Canopy bed A type of bed that has four posts extending upward. The distinct feature to the piece is the top tent-like canopy.

Cantilever A projecting beam or structure supporting only one end of a piece of furniture. It is anchored to a wall.

Case goods Furniture that is not upholstered that is used to hold or case household items.

Caster A wheel that is mounted to the bottom of a piece of furniture so that the piece can roll.

Chaise longue A French term meaning a chair that has been stretched out in its design.

Cherry Hardwood from North America that is medium brown in color with a straight to medium grain pattern. Used in furniture and cabinet construction.

Chesser A style of furniture that combines a dresser and chest in one piece. Typically, it will have a narrow vertical run of drawers on one side and a smaller set of drawers with a mirror on the other.

Chest A piece of furniture that features a series of drawers; it is usually a narrow piece.

Chesterfield A sofa style that features a low back and arms, which are at the same level.

Chest-on-chest A piece of furniture that has an upper and lower set of drawers and that is built in two pieces.

Chiffonier Typically, a narrow chest of drawers; also known as a lingerie chest.

Chippendale (1750–1790) A style of furniture; the name comes from Thomas Chippendale, who was a cabinetmaker and designer. He published his designs in *The Gentleman and Cabinet-Maker's Direction* in 1754. He incorporated many different influences into his designs, and an original Chippendale is one of the most sought-after types of furniture for antique collectors today.

Claw and ball A foot detail in which a bird talon is grasping a ball. This style of leg is found on many Chippendale-style pieces.

Colonial (1700–1780) A style that combines the elements of William and Mary, Queen Anne, and Chippendale to create a simplified style.

Commode A French word meaning a small chest with doors.

Contrast Something strikingly unlike the rest of a piece of work in form, line, or color; for example, a piece of furniture that uses two different wood materials such as maple, which is light in color, and purple heart, which has a deep purple tone.

Corbel Typically, a carved right-angled piece of wood that is used to support a top surface.

Corner cupboard Also known as a corner cabinet, this piece is designed to fit into the corner of a room.

Cornice The top finish molding to a column.

Craftsman An individual trained in furniture construction or other trades. The term can also mean the Craftsman style, which refers to the Arts and Crafts style. *See also* Arts and Crafts.

Credenza A sideboard; today, credenzas are used as filing cabinets.

Curio cabinet A piece that has glass shelves and doors for display; it is typically a narrow piece.

Curvilinear Round and curving forms that tend to imply flowing shapes; example: a round pedestal table with a turned base.

D

Dentil molding A molding detail that has a blocking design in it, creating a.solid and void look of a geometric square.

Dinette A small table and chairs used in a kitchen nook.

Direction Movement created by the placement of shapes in a design; for example, a tall bookcase will have a vertical direction, whereas a long dining table can have a horizontal direction.

Distressed A furniture detail in which the piece is made to look old by creating marks, dents, and chips in it, giving the piece the appearance of an antique.

Dominant Usually the largest shape or group of shapes in a design; for example, in a bedroom, the bed is the dominant piece.

Dovetail A type of joinery usually found in drawer construction. The name comes from the fact that the interlocking fingers cut into the wood look like a dove's tail.

Dowel Round wooden pegs that are inserted into drilled holes in order to connect two pieces. This type of joinery is used in mass-production furniture.

Dresser A piece of furniture that typically has sets of drawers vertically and horizontally and is a low piece, about 30 to 36 inches tall. Many designs also have a mirror that attaches to the dresser.

Drop-in seat Also known as a slip seat, in which the upholstered seat fits into an open chair frame and can be removed easily.

Drop leaf A type of table that has hinged leaves that can be raised or lowered to increase the overall tabletop size.

Drop seat A concave seat in which the front and middle have been carved out from a solid piece of wood, such as a Windsor chair.

E

Early American (1640–1700) A style that is basic and utilitarian. This New World furniture was made from local woods but was based on European styles from England, France, and Spain.

Ebony Hardwood from Africa that is black in color. Typically used as an accent or inlay because of its high cost.

Eclectic The process of mixing design styles, eras, or tones to create a unique style to the room or set of furniture.

Eight-way hand tied The manner in which a spring seat on upholstered furniture is tied together. Each spring is tied in eight different directions, creating a seat that acts like a complete unit instead of individual springs.

Elizabethan (1558–1603) A style of furniture named after Queen Elizabeth I of England; this was not a unified classic style, but many pieces have an architectural quality to them.

Embossing Stamping a design into wood to give the look of carving.

Emphasis The principle of design that stresses one feature as being the center around which the rest of the design is coordinated, for example, a carving on the top of a bonnet top armoire that creates a focal point to the piece.

Empire (1800–1840) A style of furniture from France that has dark finishes with graceful lines and strong proportions, creating a solid look and feel to the furniture.

End matching Two pieces of veneer are lined up at the end grain to create one continuous grain pattern.

Entertainment center A large piece of furniture designed to house entertainment equipment such as a TV and audio and visual components.

Ergonomics The study of human dimensions as they relate to design, which is essential to creating functional furniture.

Escutcheon The back plate to a knob, bail, or keyhole on a piece of furniture.

F

Fancy-faced veneers Veneers that are cut into patterns to add detail and interest to a surface.

Fauteuil A French upholstered open armchair.

Federal (1780–1820) A furniture style that combines both Hepplewhite and Sheraton styles, using straight clean lines, tapered legs, and inlay.

Fiberboard A man-made material made from compressed wood fibers and glue; typically known as MDF (medium-density fiberboard).

Fiddle back A design for the back of a chair that has the shape of a fiddle or violin.

Finger joint A type of joinery in which equal amounts of material are removed from two pieces of wood so that they will interlock with one another.

Finial The top detail of a post; this piece is typically turned and is common on four-poster beds.

Fluting A grouping of carved-out grooves that creates an architectural detail to the furniture.

Form The actual shape and structure of an object.

Four poster A type of bed that has four posts extending upward. These posts are typically a tall distinct feature to the piece.

Fretwork Decorative woodwork found on furniture and architecture, such as in Victorian homes.

Futon A foldable sofa/bed that uses a single large cushion.

G

Gateleg table A style of drop leaf table in which an extra leg swings out like a gate to support each leaf when it is raised.

Georgian (1714–1760) A style of furniture named after

Kings George I and II of England. This style is a more ornate version of the Queen Anne style. It has larger proportions, carving, and cabriole legs with a pad or ball and claw foot.

Gestalt A unified configuration or pattern of visual elements whose properties cannot be derived from a simple summation of its parts.

Gestures Two-dimensional and three-dimensional drawings used to convey ideas quickly; this is a good way to create quick rough ideas.

Gilding A finishing technique in which a thin layer of gold or a similar metal is applied over the base material.

Glaze A technique in the finishing process that changes the tone of the color while highlighting the grain of the material.

Gold leaf A finishing technique in which thin sheets of gold-like material are applied to the base material; the same practice using silver is called silver leaf.

Gothic (1150–1550, revived in the nineteenth century) An architectural style that has influenced furniture design. The most recognizable element from the era is the Gothic arc, which is an arc that creates a pointed top.

Grain A pattern in wood caused by the growth rings of the tree. Grain patterns are different for different species of tree. The grain pattern also can be different depending on whether the lumber is through-and-through cut or quartersawn cut.

H

Headboard The back portion of a bed. It can be used with a cleat to attach it to the wall or with a footboard and rail to create a complete bed.

HDF High-density fiberboard, or Masonite, is an engineered product using wood fibers, creating harder, denser material than MDF that is used to create flat sheet goods. *See also* LDF and MDF.

Hepplewhite (1765–1800) A style of furniture named after George Hepplewhite, whose designs were published in *The Cabinet-Maker and Upholsterer's Guide* in 1788. The features of this furniture include delicate elements such as tapered legs, veneers, and inlay.

Hickory Hardwood from North America that is cream to brown in color with dark brown streaks running with the grain.

Hierarchy A group of things arranged in order of rank, grade, class, and so on; for example, a set of dining chairs, in which the armchairs at the ends of the table would be a higher rank than the side chairs.

Highboy A piece of furniture with a set of drawers running vertically and legs at the base, creating a light visual feel. It typically will have cabriole legs and a traditional style.

High relief A type of carving that is similar to bas relief but is deeper and creates more of a three-dimensional feel.

Hutch A piece of furniture with a buffet-style base, sometimes on legs, with open shelving on top for displaying dishes and platters.

I

Inlay A design technique in which contrasting woods or other materials are set into a groove in the material, creating a contrasting flush surface.

J

Jacobean (1603–1690) A style of furniture that comes from England upon which early American furniture was modeled. It has dark finishes and mixes straight lines with ornate carving.

K

KD Knock down; the furniture comes disassembled when delivered. Also known as RTA (ready-to-assemble) furniture. *See also* RTA.

Kiln-dried Wood that has been dried in large ovens by slowly increasing the temperature to reduce the moisture in the lumber. All lumber that is sold to the public has been kiln-dried.

L

Lacquer A clear top coat finish that protects the base coat and color of the piece.

Ladder-back chairs Chairs with wide horizontal back slats creating a ladder-style design. These chairs were made popular by the Shaker style of furniture.

Laminate A thin piece of material used as the finish surface such as plastic, metal, or melamine that is glued to the base material.

Lattice A criss-cross wood pattern in which strips of wood are attached perpendicular to one another.

Leather The hide of an animal that is used in upholstery and other types of furniture.

Line A visual element of length, created by setting a point in motion.

Load-bearing The part of a structure on which the weight is carried; for example, the load-bearing structure for a table is the legs because they are what supports the weight of the piece.

Louis XIII (1610–1643) French furniture that has a massive, heavy feel and look to it, with carving and turning. It was influenced by designs from Italy and Spain.

Louis XIV (1643–1715) A style of furniture based on the Louis XIII style. This era in France featured extravagant living by the royalty and the upper class. One main style feature is the X-style stretcher to the chairs and other pieces.

Louis XV (1715–1774) An era of social change in France that was a transitional period for furniture styles as well. The early years were influenced by the Louis XIV style, so details like the X-style stretcher were used.

Louis XVI (1774–1789) A style of furniture in which the curved lines of the legs were changed and became rigid turned details, whereas the backs of chairs had simple ovals and circles.

Love seat A small sofa designed for two persons.

Lyre back A style of a chair back that resembles a harp.

M

Mahogany Hardwood from Africa, known as African mahogany, and from Latin America, known as Honduras or Genuine mahogany, which is light pink to reddish-brown in color with a straight grain.

Major axis A line of reference around which a form or composition is balanced; for example, the major axis on a long dining table is the horizontal surface plane.

Maple Hardwood from North America that is light blond in color with a straight to medium grain pattern. Used in furniture, cabinets, and floor construction. Other species of maple include bird's eye, country, curly, hard, quilted, soft, and spalted maple.

Mass Bulk, size, magnitude; for example, a trunk-style coffee table has different mass than a coffee table that has four legs with negative space under it.

MDF Medium-density fiberboard is an engineered product using softwood fibers, wax, and resin to create flat sheet goods. This product is associated with health risks because it uses a formaldehyde resin. Also available in low and high densities. *See also* LDF and HDF.

Mid-Century Modern (1940–1960) The Modern style can arguably be said to have started early in the twentieth century or even earlier, with the Michael Thonet chair No. 14 (1859). The Industrial Revolution made it possible to mass produce furniture. The Bauhaus continued with the mass production of steel-designed furniture pre–World War II.

Minor axis A line of reference around a lesser subdominant or subordinate part of the composition; for example, the minor axis on a long dining table is the vertical legs.

Mission A style of furniture that is a rebellion against Victorian industrialism. This is handcrafted furniture that emphasizes construction by using the joinery as a major design element. This style is also known as Arts and Crafts style. *See also* Arts and Crafts.

Modernist Twentieth-century furniture based on function that creates a clean contemporary design. It also used manufacturing to create mass-produced furniture.

Modular design Units of standardized sizes or designs that can be arranged together in a variety of ways.

Molding A decorative detail to furniture including base molding and crown molding as well as an overlay onto flat surfaces.

Mortise and tenon A type of joinery that attaches two perpendicular pieces. The first piece will have a mortise (square opening) cut into the wood, and the second piece is a tenon (notched out piece of wood). The tenon slides into the mortise, creating a tight strong joint.

N

Negative space Unoccupied areas or empty space.

Nest of tables A table set containing tables of decreasing sizes in which one table can slide under the next.

O

Oak Hardwood from North America that is light to medium brown in color with a wide grain pattern. This wood is used in furniture, cabinet, and floor construction. Quartersawn oak is used in Arts and Crafts furniture.

Occasional table A small style of table also known as an end or cocktail table.

Ogee A style of edge that is double-curved, in which one curve is concave and the next is convex. Commonly found on tabletop edges or door details.

Ottoman An upholstered seat or footstool that does not have arms or a back.

Overlay Material applied to a flat surface of wood. It is typically a trim piece.

P

Padauk Hardwood from Africa that has a straight grain that is orange to red in color with dark strips in the grain.

Panel The center floating part of a cabinet door that is held in place by the stile and rail.

Patina A process that changes the outside surface through aging, oxidizing, or rubbing.

Pedestal table A table with a single center support.

Pediment A triangular architectural style detail that crowns the top of a bed or an armoire.

Pennsylvania Dutch (1729–1830) A simple, straight, clean-line style of furniture based on function. Many of these pieces feature light to dark brown stains or colorful folk painting.

Pie crust table Typically, a small round side or pedestal table with a raised carved detailed edge.

Pilgrim (1550–1600) Functional American furniture influenced by England.

Pine Softwood from North America that is light yellow with a deep yellow to light brown grain.

Pineapple A carved detail found on early-nineteenth-century American and English bedposts that was modeled on a pineapple.

Plane A flat surface; for example, a tabletop surface.

Plinth A squared-off base of a piece of furniture; in architecture, it is commonly found at the base of a column.

Plywood A man-made material created by prying wood sheets off a log and then layering them so that the grain of each ply runs perpendicular to the next. Typical thicknesses for furniture construction are ¼ inch, ½ inch, and ¾ inch.

Pocket door A type of door that can open and slide into a cabinet by using specially designed hardware that basically incorporates a concealed hinge and drawer slide into one piece of hardware.

Polyurethane A synthetic product used to create the foam material in cushions. It is also a clear coat material used in the finishing process as a top coat.

Positive space Space that the object occupies.

Proportion The relationship between the parts of a whole in terms of size; for example, a large table can appear lighter by using tapered legs, or a small table can appear heavy by thickening the legs.

Purple heart Hardwood from Latin America that is purple in color with a straight grain.

Q

Quartersawn A type of lumber-cutting process in which the log is cut into quarters before turning it into lumber.

Quatrefoil A detail ornamental figure that is divided into four equal curves. It is used as an appliqué or carved into the surface.

Queen Anne (1700–1755) A style of furniture that gets its name from Queen Anne of England (1702–1714). This type of furniture is still popular today. One main element to this furniture is the cabriole legs, which create a light, graceful feel.

R

Rail The horizontal structural frame of a cabinet door.

Rake Legs that are angled or slanted so that they are not vertical.

Reclining chair An upholstered chair; the back of the chair will angle back.

Rectilinear Composed of straight lines; for example, a square end table with straight tapered legs.

Reeding The opposite of a fluting detail; long beaded lines are added to the surface.

Refectory table A long table with heavy legs and stretchers.

Renaissance (1460–1600, revived in the 19th century) A style of furniture; originated in Italy and was a reaction to the Gothic style. The furniture is functional with carving and scroll work. The revival pieces from 1850 to 1880 used the same details and were typically made from walnut.

Repetition Using the same visual elements over and over within the same composition; for example, a veneer design within a door that is used throughout a series of pieces such as a bedroom set.

Rhythm Flow or movement characterized by basically regular recurrence of elements or features.

Ribband-back A style of chair that has a back detail resembling an entwined ribbon. Many Chippendale-style chairs have this detail.

Rococo A style that came from France in the early eighteenth century; it influenced architecture and furniture design.

Rolltop desk A desk that has a front slatted panel that can be rolled down and locked to protect the interior compartments.

RTA Ready to assemble; furniture that comes disassembled when delivered. It is also known as KD (knockdown) furniture. *See also* KD.

Rush seat A style of seat that uses either natural cattail leaf rush, bulrush, or man-made paper fiber rush. It is woven into a pattern forming four distinct triangles in the seat.

S

Scale Size relative to a constant standard or measure related to human dimension; for example, ¼ scale means that each ¼ inch on the drawing equals 1 foot in real space.

Scandinavian design (1930–1950) A style of furniture from Denmark and Sweden. This design has also been called contemporary and typically uses natural woods and veneers.

Secretary A desk with a drop-down writing surface and drawers below.

Settee A small bench or sofa.

Shaker (1820–1860) A simple functional style from the United States. Some common details are tapered legs, ladder-back chairs with contrasting woven seats, and simple wooden knobs.

Shape The two-dimensional contour that characterizes an object or area, in contrast to three-dimensional form.

Sheraton (1780–1820) A style of furniture named after Thomas Sheraton, whose designs were published in *The Cabinet Maker and Upholsterer's Drawing Book* in 1791. This neoclassical furniture has straight lines and contrasting veneers and was widely produced in the United States.

Sideboard A piece of furniture used in the dining room; similar to a buffet table.

Silver leaf A finishing technique in which thin sheets of silver-like material are applied to the base material; the same practice using gold is called gold leaf.

Sinuous springs Also known as zigzag springs; a wire attaches to the rails inside an upholstered piece to create a spring effect to the seat or back. *See also* zigzag springs.

Skirt On upholstered furniture, this is the material that hangs down at the bottom edge, hiding the legs.

Slat-back chair A chair designed with a back made from vertical pieces of wood.

Slip match Veneer is used by slipping sheets into a pattern such as a diamond or sunburst.

Slip seat Also known as a drop-in seat; the upholstered seat fits into an open chair frame and can be easily removed.

Sofa A wide upholstered piece of furniture that creates seating for at least three persons.

Sofa table A narrow table designed to sit behind the back of a sofa.

Solid Having no breaks or divisions.

Space Distance extending in all directions, including both the positive space of the furniture and the negative space in the room.

Spindle A turned piece of wood that is typically used for the backs of chairs.

Spiral leg A type of leg that is carved to have a twist or spiral.

Spring cushion A cushion that contains coil springs and is wrapped in foam, batting, and material.

Staining A step in the finishing process where color is applied to the piece. Typically, stains are available in an alcohol, oil, or water base.

Stile The vertical structural frame of a cabinet door.

Stretcher A support that is attached to the leg base of furniture, such as chairs and tables.

Stripping The process of removing the existing finish on a piece of furniture.

Stylized Changing an existing image by using its shape or form as a starting point. This can be used to create artwork for carved details on furniture.

Subdominant Second degree of importance. Smaller than dominant shapes and forms and working as supporting elements in a composition; for example, in a bedroom, the dresser is the subdominant piece.

Subordinate The smallest element in a design, sometimes referred to as an accent; for example, in a bedroom, the nightstand is the subordinate piece.

Subtractive space To construct by continually removing material; for example, carving into wood.

Swivel chair A style of chair that revolves from side to side from a fixed point such as a base.

Symmetrical Equal-sized and equal-spaced shapes based off a central axis.

T

Tactile texture A texture that can be seen and felt; for example, a carved detail on the edge of a tabletop.

Tapered leg A leg that is cut so that it is smaller toward the bottom.

Teak Hardwood from Asia that is medium brown in color. This wood is typically used in outdoor furniture and boat construction because the natural oils in the wood protect it from the elements.

Tension Forces that affect elements of furniture by pushing out or pulling in, affecting balance or counter-balance.

Tongue and groove A type of joinery in which the edge of the wood has a channel (groove) cut into it and then a tab (tongue) cut into the other side. This allows all the pieces to continually connect together. This style of joinery is used in wood floors as well as furniture.

Trestle table A style of table that is designed so that each side acts as a brace to support the weight of the top.

Trompe l'oeil French for "trick the eye"; a painting process that creates three-dimensional images on flat surfaces such as furniture and walls.

Trundle bed A style of bed that is good for small spaces because it is two beds that take up the space of one; the lower bed slides under the top bed when not in use.

Turned A style of leg produced with a lathe that allows material to be removed while it spins. The material starts as a block, and a cutting tool removes material to create the final design.

U

Unity A grouping that is a union of related parts; for example, the same type of foot detail used in a living room set on the armoire, end tables, and sofas.

Upholstery Furniture that has been covered in material such as fabric, leather, or other soft materials.

V

Value A measure of relative lightness or darkness.

Variety A different form of the same item, material, and so on.

Veneer Wood that has been peeled off the tree in thin sheets. It is available in different species and sizes, commonly in sizes of 4 feet by 8 feet and 2 feet by 8 feet.

Victorian (1840–1910) A style of furniture named after Queen Victoria of England (1837–1901). This was the beginning of the machine age, thus allowing for the first mass production of furniture.

Visual flow Designed to move the viewer's eye from one point to another.

Visual texture An implied texture that is not tactile; for example, the grain in wood, such as zebrawood or curly maple, can appear to be textured.

Vitrine A piece of furniture that typically has a glass top and sides and is used for displaying items. Usually end table size.

Void Unoccupied space.

Volume The total amount of space the furniture occupies.

W

Wainscoting An interior architectural detail in which wood is added in a rail, stile, and panel form at the lower half of a wall.

Walnut Hardwood from North America that is dark brown in color with a straight, wide grain pattern.

Webbing A support system in upholstered furniture in which strips of material are woven in between one another to add spring to cushions.

Wengé Hardwood from Africa that has a straight grain that is dark brown to black in color.

William and Mary (1690–1725) Named for King William and Queen Mary of England (1689–1694), this style of furniture typically features turned legs with a ball foot detail and is made from walnut.

Windsor chair A type of chair with rounded spindles forming the back of the chair and turned legs and stretchers.

Wingback chair An upholstered chair that has sides that are wing shaped at the top of the chair.

X

X-axis Horizontal direction.

X-chair A Roman-influenced chair with a distinctive "X" shape that runs from the base, creating the seat that turns into the arm.

X-style stretcher A detail made popular during the Louis XIV era. It is a stretcher that connects the legs diagonally near their base.

Y

Y-axis Vertical direction.

Yorkshire chair Also known as a wheat back chair; typically made from oak, the chair has turned front legs and stretchers and is designed as both an armchair and a side chair.

Z

Z-axis Depth.

Zebrawood Hardwood from Africa that has a straight grain of multiple tones of light to black, creating a contrasting zebra-like color to the wood; because of its high cost, it is typically found in veneer form.

Zigzag springs A type of spring used in the upholstery process. Also known as sinuous springs. *See also* sinuous springs.

Index